# HOW TO

# HYGGE

## The Secrets of Nordic Living

Signe Johansen

bluebird
books for life

# Contents

# Introduction

**Hello and welcome! Or, *Hei, og velkommen!***

Make yourself at home. Perhaps put the kettle on for a cuppa, or pour yourself a Scotch and curl up somewhere you can be left undisturbed for a little while. The world of Nordic hygge awaits.

'What exactly *is* hygge?' you ask.

A Danish/Norwegian word that translates as a feeling of cosiness, hygge can also mean kinship and conviviality. If mindfulness is about the self and looking inward, hygge is about being sociable and looking outward; it's about taking pleasure in the simple things in life, in fellowship with kith and kin.

In fact, hygge neatly encapsulates everything that is great about Nordic living. One caveat, though: as a word it doesn't really exist in Finnish or Swedish, so I freely admit I've used creative licence in applying the word to the region as a whole, to explore why we live so well.

In recent years, Denmark, Finland, Iceland, Norway and Sweden have topped so many quality-of-life studies that it's almost become a running joke among bemused locals. Yet life in the region is often reduced to a series of tired clichés: everyone's blonde (including the furniture—thanks for that, IKEA), we love pickled herring and meatballs, Abba is our greatest (musical) export along with the Swedish Chef from *The Muppet Show*.

Our interiors are all crisply white, and we only wear clothes in a monochrome palette of grey, grey and … more grey. If you watch any Nordic noir programmes you'd be forgiven for thinking coffee is consumed by the litre, not by the cupful. There is a nugget of truth in that last caricature: in lists of the highest coffee consumption per capita, the Nordic region regularly features near the top. We're amped up on caffeine, but then arguably you have to be when it's so dark and chilly outside most of the year.

Don't get me wrong, Nordic life is not perfect. Humans everywhere have their quirks and idiosyncrasies; we're no exception.

We just have a different perspective on living. After all, we may be your north-eastern cousins, yet it seems at times the way we live is a world apart; therefore this book explores the context of Nordic living, how we operate. Think of this as a light-hearted primer for how to live your life to the fullest, not a bible to be slavishly followed. Adopt as many or as few as you fancy of the suggestions given here, but in truth there are no hard-and-fast rules on hygge. It's as much a feeling as a cultural concept.

I asked Diana Henry, one of the UK's foremost food writers, to share her thoughts on hygge:

'As soon as I arrived in Copenhagen—on a dark night in December—I understood the concept of hygge, even though I didn't have a word for it. Dragging our cases towards our hotel we noticed candles everywhere, tall fat ones in grand windows, little tea lights in smaller windows. Copenhagen was lit by a series of gentle glows. How kind, I thought, that the people in all these hotels and restaurants and apartments care enough to create warmth for everyone around them. The next day, the candles were there again, and not just at night, but in the little café where we ate cinnamon buns and wrapped our hands around mugs of coffee mid-morning, and in the restaurant where we had open sandwiches at lunchtime. By the time I left I knew what the candles were about. Perhaps because they have more hours of darkness than us, Nordics have learnt to deal with it, and with the cold too. Candlelight is one of their antidotes to darkness, but warm jumpers, great food and drink and a concern to make a good home are all part of it. I understood it—hygge, cosiness, a delight in life, the love of snuggling up in the corner of your sofa—and wished very much that we had it too. I think we need it.'

And that's what I reckon too. We *need* hygge in our lives.

Given my own background in the food industry, this book celebrates conviviality and togetherness. Food and drink are at the heart of hygge, and I was fortunate to grow up in a family who came together over home-cooked meals; however, I'm not suggesting you should be a martyr in the kitchen and make everything from scratch. There are recipes here to inspire you, from quick snacks to fika treats. By simplifying your cooking skills, you can spend more time doing what you really love, or take up another valuable life skill. Many of us have a tendency to needlessly complicate everything. Resist that temptation at every opportunity—you will feel liberated, I assure you.

Nature undoubtedly sets the pace in the Nordic region. We have a healthy fear of and respect for the elements, and feel the call of the outdoors at all times of the year—a bit of bad weather never stopped the Vikings from their raids, and nor do we let it stop us today. For us, to be active is to be alive, and life takes place as much outdoors as indoors. Hygge is sometimes reduced to cake, candles and lovely soft furnishings, but to my mind it's not merely about gratuitous indulgence; to a certain extent you have to *earn* it. That doesn't mean you have to go hell for leather on the extreme-sports spectrum and punish yourself doing exercise you hate—far from it.

Small adventures in the wild are always preferable to slogging it out in a neon-lit city gym, but channelling a Nordic pragmatism means making a few compromises. Living in London—a world-class city though it may be—means I definitely have to. It's not as easy to frolic outdoors here as it was when I was growing up in Oslo, a place where you can clip on your skis and go for an hour-long spin around the neighbourhood in midwinter if you wish. The main thing to be alert to if you want to live your life to the fullest is to make the time to be active every day, no matter how miserable it is beyond your front door. Recent studies have proven that inactivity is worse for our longevity than a bit of extra blubber on our hips. The Nordic philosophy is that it's never about looking good: it's about feeling great, all year round.

Underpinning hygge is a craving for simplicity, an urge to pare everything back to basics. Jettison the anxieties and clutter of modern living to free up your time and energy to make the most of life. At the core of hygge is the guiding principle that we must all make the most of the short time we have on this planet ... And be kind to ourselves and those around us.

So whether you're fascinated by Nordic noir, have a penchant for great design, or you've visited the region and been captivated by the way we live, I hope *How to Hygge* proffers something for everyone.

I firmly believe anyone can benefit from a little Nordic hygge in their lives, so take a leap in and join us ...

**Signe Johansen, London 2016** —

# one

## nature &
## the seasons

# Into the Wild

'But just to keep alive is not enough. To live you must have sunshine and freedom, and a little flower to love.'

Hans Christian Andersen

'Come on,' Papa Johansen said one late May evening, interrupting my mewling about how much I hated revision for exams, 'let's go pick some lilies of the valley.'

Off we went to a nearby woodland, just up the hill from our house in Oslo. It wasn't the most accessible of slopes to pick flowers. I recall clambering my way up from a distant main road, sturdy hiking boots squelching flatulently underfoot as we ventured deeper into the woods, trying not to fall over (a common occurrence—I'm extremely clumsy).

Like any surly, borderline histrionic teenager facing a battery of exams that week, I was experiencing that crushing sense of impending doom about life, and resented my dad for badgering me into such a frivolous trek into nature. What a waste of time when I could be revising algebra! It felt like a bit of a mission to get there and I wondered how anyone would normally come across this fabled patch of flowers, either by accident or by design. Being the diligent forager my father is, he'd sniffed out this woodland a few years previously and every May he would return to pick flowers.

Yet as soon as we saw the thousands of delicate lily of the valley plants, all that exam stress and fear vaporized into thin air. Bright little scented flowers as far as the eye could see, half-shaded by the overhanging canopy of trees, the occasional dapple of twilight sunshine to illuminate their long leaves and pretty snowcrop-shaped flowers. Dad and I just looked at each other giddy with glee and spent a good half hour picking as many flowers as we could carry. The field was so abundant with them that we could have decorated our entire neighbourhood with lilies and there would still have been plenty left over.

With its elegant freshness *Convallaria majalis* really is that 'little flower to love'. It's hardly a coincidence that lily of the valley is so redolent of happy memories for us as a family; not only do I have those teenage woodland memories to call on when the relentless pace of London starts to grind me down, but it's the flower my mother chose for her wedding bouquet.

As Diane Ackerman writes in *A Natural History of the Senses*, 'smell is the most direct of all our senses' and thus has the capacity to trigger the most overwhelming nostalgia. While I type this I'm wafting lily of the valley bath essence by London perfumier Floris in front of my nose (and trying not to spill it all over the place). Both my English maternal grandmother and my mother continue to use this bath essence, and I carry on the tradition in spite of the deleterious effect it has on my bank balance (one bottle has lasted nearly two years so it's still cheaper than a daily fancy coffee habit, is my reasoning). It's an olfactory trip down memory lane, and never fails to delight: lily of the valley's bright green top notes have that clean, dewy scent that symbolizes the promise of spring mixed with a musky pungency of sultry summer nights.

A spritz of this cool, fresh scent is more than an olfactory joy; it's a vital part of my connection with nature and part of a sensory map that reflects my own particular narrative in life. You will no doubt have sensory experiences that trigger a similar response, and I bet for many of you who spent time outdoors as children, teenagers and into adulthood, some of those scents will be deeply imprinted on your sensory DNA.

# Setting the Pace

To echo Ralph Waldo Emerson, nature sets the pace across the Nordic region and 'her secret is patience'. Everything that is compelling and vital about the Nordic countries, be it our food culture(s), great design, architecture, arguably even our social democratic traditions, is in some way grounded in a deep respect for nature and the elements. Rather than fight the long, dark winters we've learnt how to embrace the cold, how to prepare for it and how to find joy in being indoors when it's miserable outside—themes I'll return to in later chapters.

Hygge is about getting back to basics, about prioritizing what's important in life, and that means nothing without context and an understanding of what makes us Nordics tick. In fact, it's impossible to fully understand hygge and therefore life in general in Denmark, Finland, Iceland, Norway and Sweden without a close look at nature and the seasons and how central they are to our identity. To be Nordic is by definition to be both a keen observer of and participant in nature. We're a people who throughout history have developed strategies to cope with the stark contrasts of short, ecstatic summers and long, harsh winters. While our love of great cakes, twinkling votives and beautiful interiors is a crucial part of that, our love of '*friluftsliv*', or the slightly less evocative English rendition 'free air life', is as important a factor. Henrik Ibsen is thought to have been the first to coin this phrase in his poem '*På Viddene*', or 'On the Heights', in 1859. Its a rather long poem so I'll spare you the whole thing and share this nugget:

In the lonely mountain farm,
My abundant catch I take.
There is a hearth, and table,
And *friluftsliv* for my thoughts.

What Ibsen was suggesting, and what I suspect most Nordics will recognize, is a yearning for getting away from it all, of seeking solace in nature, preferably in a cabin far away from the nearest main road, with the odd moose or sheep here and there for company. That isn't necessarily a uniquely Nordic experience, and I'm acutely aware that this veers into stereotyping territory. What *is* distinctively Nordic is the freedom to roam in nature at any time of year, a right that is considered sacrosanct across the region. As Robert Macfarlane writes in *The Old Ways: A Journey on Foot*

*'I ... envy the Scandinavian customary right of* Allemansrätten *("Everyman's right"). This convention—born of a region that did not pass through centuries of feudalism, and therefore has no inherited deference to a landowning class—allows a citizen to walk anywhere on uncultivated land provided that he or she cause no harm; to light fires; to sleep anywhere beyond the curtilage of a dwelling; to gather flowers, nuts and berries; and to swim in any watercourse (rights to which the newly enlightened access laws of Scotland increasingly approximate).'*

It is essentially a human right to have access to nature, a benefit that is available to everyone, not just the privileged few. You don't have to own fancy, branded outdoor gear, or spend lots of money to be in nature; status doesn't matter once you're in the wild—it's the ultimate democratic ideal.

Someone asked me recently what the defining characteristics of being a Norwegian are, and I struggled to come up with a succinct

answer other than a love of skiing, cabin porn, an addiction to coffee and the invention of the paper clip. In hindsight, I should have been
a little less flippant and thought a little harder. What I would say now is
that many of us share that craving for the *friluftsliv* of being in nature that
Ibsen cites in his poem, and across the Nordic region we are proud of the
freedom to roam in the wild as enshrined in our laws which Macfarlane
identified. This doesn't mean we're solitary creatures *per se*, or that we're
in denial about modernity and exist in some sort of permanent escapist
fantasy, but we feel an intense need to escape the hustle and bustle of
modern life in order to reflect, to gather our thoughts and to gain a sense
of perspective.

According to the UN, over 50 per cent of the world's population now lives
in urban areas, and that figure is forecast to rise to 66 per cent by 2050.
While the cultural, economic, political and social opportunities afforded by

*"Nature calms you and allows you to reflect on
the very essence of what living is about."* ———

living in cities are unquestionably immense, studies also show a correlation between living in cities and a rise in mental illness, a fact that we will need to address as the world becomes more and more urbanized. The pace of our modern lives is draining us, and studies further show that in our increasingly deracinated urban existence we reap the benefits for both our mental and our physical health of switching off from work, everyday worries and, crucially, untethering ourselves from mobile phones and tablets. 'Digital detoxing' is becoming more commonplace, and what better way to disengage from the nagging notifications of your mobile phone than to head into the wilderness where WiFi is out of bounds?

I know from my own experience of living nearly a decade in London that I feel a visceral urge to get out of the city every few weeks. The sirens, the traffic, the cyclists trying to jump red lights, the strident march and tense jaws of commuters … A world-class city this may be, but it gets to a point where I physically can't tolerate it anymore and have to escape, which isn't unique to this Londoner, of course. When we lived in Norway, I could go flower-picking in the woods a few hundred metres from our house, or put on a pair of skis and go for a cross-country ski run up and around the hill after school.

Those little daily diversions from the pressure of modern life could be made much more easily, more freely. We lived in a capital city that had crystal-clear fjords, excellent ski tracks and a vast wilderness called Nordmarka within thirty minutes of the city centre. And it was just so safe. I could go into nature on my own, or with friends, and no parent ever seemed worried about paedophiles or serial killers hunting children down and doing unspeakable things to them. Other Nordic capitals share a similar urban–nature landscape that makes it easy for their citizens to be outdoors in nature at any time of the year, and that feature alone I reckon has a huge influence on the high quality of living they can offer. In the book *Happy City*, Copenhagen is cited as a model of town planning, designed so as to accommodate the needs of its residents. Wide bicycle lanes are a prime example: the city council built them in recognition of the fact that cyclists like to chat to each other as they zip around town. Small details like this make for much more liveable places.

Nature calms you, it settles you and allows you to step back and reflect on the very essence of what living is about. To my mind, if your thoughts are clouded by anxiety, fear and stress then a getaway to a green wood, a walk by the sea or a gentle hike up a mountain does more to lift the spirits than any expensive handbag or latest must-have gadget could ever do.

∞

Seeking solace in nature is at the heart of Nordic hygge

# Keep Calm & Hug a Tree:
# The Benefits of Ecotherapy

Anthropologist Margaret Mead once wrote about the 'spiritual and mental ancestors' that form our identity and, whether or not you buy into that idea, I'd wager that there is definitely a therapeutic benefit to returning to our ancestral landscape. Lest you think I'm a tree-hugging hippie, let me assure you I'm not. Every encounter with nature is one that has reaped unexpected rewards and helped to soothe any latent anxieties about school, friends and fears about the future, but I'm wary of the pseudo-spiritual and clean-living types dominating the current narrative on health and well-being. What I find continually fascinating about nature is the way it brings about a feeling of clarity, a renewed focus and sense of purpose, as well as its healing properties. Time spent in nature has profound therapeutic benefits, something most of us who spend time outdoors probably realized on an intuitive level, and the recognition of this fact is increasingly gaining traction beyond the field of 'ecotherapy'.

*'In its most basic sense, ecotherapy is about the healing and psychological benefits of being in nature and natural settings. In a modern context the links between nature and positive effects on mental health can be traced back to the early part of the last century.'*
— Martin Jordan, 'Back to Nature', *Therapy Today*, April 2009

According to a 2015 Stanford University study with the catchy title of 'Nature experience reduces rumination and subgenual prefrontal cortex activation', spending time in nature means you're less prone to brooding. Nature's nurturing properties aren't yet fully understood, but scientists and medical professionals are beginning to advocate more time spent in the great outdoors. The relationship between humans and nature has to be a reciprocal one, which means we have to know how to look after the outdoors, how to maintain it for the future. While the Vikings may have had a reputation for plunder, modern Nordics understand you can't just wander into the wild and take whatever you want from it. Even if you're completely clueless about a lot of nature's secrets you can volunteer to help maintain a garden, or a nature reserve in your local area. According to a *Guardian* report, physicians are now advising patients to spend more time gardening to improve their mental health, and gardeners have long advocated that getting one's hands dirty rummaging around in soil is good for our immune systems. Consider adopting a tree. Take part in community-led activities that teach you about nature and responsible stewardship. Baby steps can make all the difference, so don't be daunted if you live somewhere with limited access to nature and wilderness. Even looking at images of nature can have a restorative effect, something Henry David Thoreau wrote about in an essay on healthcare design in *The Atlantic* magazine way back in 1862. Patients in hospitals who had a view of trees outdoors were found to recover much faster from their illness than those who only had a wall to look at. Whether it's a photo of a waterfall, a picture of baby animals or a view of trees outside your window, nature has a near-magical ability to restore you.

In fact, UK charity Mind and the University of Essex found that the benefits of ecotherapy for mental health were substantial and applicable to everyone, regardless of whether they suffer from mental health issues. They found that time spent in nature:

∞  Boosts self-esteem
∞  Helps people with mental health problems return to work
∞  Improves physical health
∞  Reduces social isolation

What's also becoming clear are the health benefits of nature on children and adolescents, particularly when it comes to concentration at school and helping to establish good habits in their formative years. Kids who spend time in nature are more focused, better behaved and show increased levels of creativity. Be it tree-climbing or tree-hugging, we all benefit from spending time in nature as often as possible

# The Seasons: Listless Insomnia & Long Hibernation

*Det finnes ikke dårlig vær—bare dårlige klær*
(No such thing as bad weather—only bad clothing)

Another key aspect of the Nordic love of nature is to never let bad weather get in the way of venturing outdoors. Except, of course, when there's a serious weather warning. We're talking the miserable end of the clement weather spectrum. Minus 20°C is the limit for cold, anything lower than that and you'd better invest in some arctic weatherproof gear. It's common sense, though: no matter whether it's raining, snowing or looking grey and blah outside, you have to get out.

While we're famous for our long, dark winters, those outside of the Nordic region are often surprised to hear that midsummer is celebrated with as much gusto as Christmas. Brief though Nordic summers may be, they are enchanting, and we need the winter months to fully appreciate summer's spectacular fecundity. Most Nordic children will have some memory of summers spent eating intensely flavoured berries, enriched thanks to the long hours of midsummer sunshine. Fjords shimmering indigo. Games played in the woods, long hikes with family and/or friends. We also go a bit crazy at midsummer, and the outdoors is our playground. Bonfires are lit, wild flowers are picked, and people gather for large parties that never seem to end. The annual festival of *Sankt Hans* is a celebration of surviving winter, and of making the most of the short summer. To my mind, Norwegian painter Nikolai Astrup best portrayed that restless energy of Nordic midsummer celebrations with vivid depictions of bold, orange fires set against a viridian mountainscape; people gathering; music flowing. Astrup identified that midsummer rapture as a quintessentially Norwegian (and by extension Nordic) trait, which we still celebrate nearly a century after he painted those images.

Most Nordics will have some story to tell of magical midsummer days and nights, when they were slightly delirious with sleep deprivation. In my experience, those days were filled with activities like playing hide and seek in the woods, foraging for wild strawberries in secret nooks dotted around the Aurland valley on the west coast of Norway, making crowns from wild flowers to put in our hair and splashing about in the ice-cold fjord nearby. In the evening, food brought us all together again. Friends and visitors would drop by, while Papa J barbecued the crayfish he'd caught that day in the fjord. Or my grandmother would fire up every hob available and, like the best line cook in a restaurant kitchen, sauté local mountain trout—enough for twenty people!—frying each fillet in fresh farmhouse butter and making a simple sauce of lemon, sour cream and dill. Who needed a restaurant when you had perfection like this at home? The grandchildren would always get stuck in and help lay the table, dress the salads, make desserts with the berries we had picked that day, and then we would join the grown-ups for these long evening feasts.

∞

Midsummer is a time of celebration, when we go a bit crazy & the outdoors is our playground

It rarely mattered what the weather was like: days and nights were to be spent outdoors as much as possible.

The Nordic way of life is simple: because we eat well and remain active all year round no matter what the weather is like, we can then treat ourselves to those delicious buns and cakes, soft furnishings and pretty votives. Hygge isn't about gratuitous indulgence. All those clichés about how wholesome Scandinavians are have a kernel of truth to them—we live healthy by choosing a sustainable solution to wellbeing, and largely ignore the faddy diets that advocate extreme detoxes or cutting out entire food groups. Our philosophy is that you can't be healthy if you're always anxious about food, about your body, and about life in general. The Vikings and Norse mythology taught us that life could be harsh and you couldn't really predict anything with certainty, so we evolved into a people who lived for the moment, and that meant making the most of each season. We therefore value fresh air over the gym, and seek out food with flavour over calorie-counting. Yes, we eat cream and butter, and we love chocolate and cake, but we only eat these foods occasionally and balance out any sweet treats with increased activity, mostly outdoors.

The emphasis on conviviality, and the coming together of family and friends were constant themes when I was growing up, no matter what

season it was. Summers, in particular, were such an idyllic time for us because we spent so many hours rejoicing in the heart of nature. And winter is all about the thrill of skiing, ice-skating, sledging in the snow and then curling up indoors with slow-cooked pork belly, freshly baked cardamom twists and endless cups of hot cocoa, or a cocktail. Whether it's light or dark outside, we know how to make the most of each season. Here's some practical advice on how you can too …

# How to Hygge in Nature

Admittedly, most of this is common sense but you'd be surprised how often I come across city slickers who have absolutely no idea about nature and the outdoors, so I'm operating on the assumption that you're an expert at navigating urban streets, but perhaps not so skilled in dealing with forest paths.

Let's start with the basics: always be prepared. Do your homework: check the weather forecast before venturing outdoors. No matter what time of year it is, you'll find that a couple of layers are essential, especially if you're traipsing around northern Europe in the summer season—it can get rainy and snow still caps the mountains even in midsummer. Invest in a pair of comfortable outdoor boots that are sturdy and have a good grip so you don't slip and slide down hills. I have a pair of Timberland boots that are now nearly twenty years old (vintage!) and they still do the job extremely well. Fully charge your mobile phone before you set off, and a Swiss army knife is always useful.

A hip flask is handy for an uplifting dram while out and about, and some delicious fika goodies won't go amiss either. Impromptu outdoor picnics are all the better for a blanket to sit on but if need be just improvise with jackets or plastic bags. A decent rucksack, preferably waterproof is ideal. Don't go crazy buying something fancy that costs an arm and a leg. You want something durable and sensible—nature doesn't care if you own the latest branded fashion accessory. The main thing is to invest carefully in a few useful items that will stand the test of time.

I grew up in a country in which there is no shame in making a simple open sandwich to take with you we call this a *'matpakke'*, or rather more prosaically a 'food package', which shows how frustrating an exercise it can sometimes be translating into English. A lingering fondness for the classic sandwich of ham and cheese with lots of mustard, crunchy lettuce and pickles stems from those childhood years in Norway, but truth be told a good slice of bread with some salted butter and indecent amounts of cheese tastes just as delicious as an elaborate sandwich when you've been larking about in the fresh air for a few hours.

Steer clear of any ingredients that might leave your sandwich soggy (cucumbers, I'm looking at you) and any ingredients that might serve as bacterial breeding grounds if exposed to heat and sun, such as mayonnaise or cream. Unless you can be bothered to bring a cool bag, seafood doesn't really do well either, and can prove to be a malodorous choice as *matpakke* fare.

Most of the salad and vegetable recipes listed in this book will serve as light nourishment to have on your adventures in nature, and more importantly that means you can save room for fika such as:

∞ The Muffins on pages 71, 75 and 88
∞ Chocolate, Almond & Marzipan Prunes on page 89
∞ Darkness & Light Cake on page 83
∞ Brown Butter, Sugar & Malt Shortbread on page 76
∞ Cardamom Twists on page 68

And the other cakes in the fika chapter can also be sliced up and packed in a sealed container, but their glazing makes for sticky fingers and can attract ants and other wildlife, so you might want to keep it simple and stick to the suggestions mentioned above. After ski races in Oslo, we kids were always handed a cardamom bun, a clementine and a juice box and nothing tasted better after a cross-country trek up and down the hills. Try not to overcomplicate things—everything tastes delicious after a few hours spent outdoors.

Whatever you do steer clear of those horrible so-called 'healthy' treats that value virtue over flavour. There's a reason why great cooks don't consider the sweet potato a stellar baking ingredient. If you're going to eat a muffin, eat the best possible muffin made with decent baking ingredients, and give the 'clean-eating' alternatives a wide berth. There is simply no hygge to be found in a flavourless mush comprising chia seeds, dates and avocado.

A flask of tea, coffee or the Boozy, Malty, Creamy Hot Chocolate on page 147 is always a welcome treat when you're out and about. Not only is it more economical than relying on random catering options, but you can control what you put in your flask (booze!).

Hygge is often social so if those closest to you aren't all that into the outdoors, consider leaving them. I'm kidding. Sort of.

But seriously, if you're hankering after some outdoor hygge and your family or friends aren't enthused by the idea, then consider joining local clubs or societies with people who love nature and the outdoors, and plan your leisure time/holidays around those outdoor excursions. At the risk of sounding like a tourist board for the Nordic countries, I can recommend a holiday in the region. Look into wilderness festivals that allow you to join a party outdoors during the warmer months. Or consider booking a cabin in a secluded area of natural beauty.

As mentioned earlier in this chapter, the manifold health benefits of getting into nature are now increasingly recognized. It's with good reason people in cities spend a lot of time in a park or square during the working week and at the weekends, but if you have the time and inclination, get out of the city, or your local town, as often as possible. The Germans have a great expression for this: *'Wir fahren ins Blaue'*, which literally means 'We're travelling into the blue' and implies that there is no clear destination or purpose to your journey; it's simply about getting out, enjoying the scenery and discovering something new.

While writing this chapter, it's been unseasonably cold in London but that hasn't stopped me from taking daily walks around the squares of Bloomsbury to clear my head. Even at dusk when it was a chilly 4°C and drizzling, I threw a woollen jumper over my top, snuggled up in a large scarf and warm coat, and went for a brisk twenty-minute jaunt around Russell Square. The result? A pleasing flush of the cheeks, but more importantly a sense of calm and ordering of my thoughts. You'll find that you sleep better when you've had some fresh air in the evening.

We're conditioned to push ourselves more and more, to take up triathlons or challenging races but being active outside in nature is a worthwhile goal in itself—there's no need to always chase the latest fashionable fitness trend, a theme I'll return to in the next chapter. Introduce children to nature at a young age: in *barnehage* (kindergarten) we had lessons outdoors and learnt about the surrounding plants and wildlife. To this day I have a mild obsession with fiddlehead ferns as a result of sitting outside during one of those lessons and learning about these strange prehistoric plants. Plus the name fiddlehead fern has to be a contender for best plant name ever.

I'm no advocate of hot-housing children at a young age when they could be playing and exploring, but children *are* inquisitive and it seems a pity

—

not to introduce a few gentle educational lessons outdoors when they're ready. Much like cooking is a great way to teach scientific fundamentals, nature can teach children about the importance of symbiosis in an ecosystem and our relationship with the environment. You don't have to go all Mensa on them and start demanding whether they can spot the Fibonacci sequence in plants and testing them on geometry (though as a kid who struggled with maths I now recognize how useful those lessons would have been in my teen years). Even just taking some plain paper and crayons or coloured pencils along on a walk through the wilderness will allow children to see patterns and absorb the beauty of nature, while exploring their creative side.

Nurture your children in nature; teach them about risk and about adventure and about facing their fears—that's the Nordic way.

# Bringing Nature's Hygge Indoors

If you're a fan of social media then make a concerted effort to follow nature, outdoor, gardening and landscape blogs, writers and photographers. Indoor plants may have again become fashionable of late on social media, but they are a timeless addition to any hygge home, a subject we'll return to in the chapter on design.

I decided to follow more of these interiors, outdoors and plant-focused accounts recently and feel so much better looking at an image of a succulent plant, a photo of the *aurora borealis* in the Arctic and cabins in the Canadian wilderness, than photos of shoes, or some fitness/lifestyle guru showing off her lithe physique while doing a yoga handstand and wearing overpriced Lycra.

One of the best investments you can make to create an atmosphere of naturally Nordic hygge is to take a long hard look at your domestic space. This is a topic I'll return to in more detail later in the book but suffice it to say that there are a few tricks you can easily employ to get your nature fix at home:

>> Start by applying the Japanese KonMari method and ask yourself if the objects you already own spark joy. If they don't, ditch 'em. Be ruthless—a cluttered living space only leads to a cluttered mind.

>> Once you've stripped back your domestic space to the items you really love and cherish, invest in a variety of houseplants. According to NASA, the best indoor plants for purifying the air include:

∞ Dwarf Date Palm (*Phoenix robelenii*)

∞ Boston Fern (*Nephrolepis exaltata*)

∞ Kimberley Queen Fern (*Nephrolepis obliterata*)

∞ Spider Plant (*Chlorophytum comosum*)

∞ Chinese Evergreen (*Aglaonema modestum*)

∞ Bamboo Palm (*Chamaedorea seifrizii*)

∞ Weeping Fig (*Ficus benjamina*)

∞ Devil's Ivy (*Epipremnum aureum*)

∞ Flamingo Lily (*Anthurium andraeanum*)

∞ Lilyturf (*Liriope spicata*)

∞ Broadleaf Lady Palm (*Rhapis excelsa*)

∞ Barberton Daisy (*Gerbera jamesonii*)

∞ Cornstalk Dracaena (*Dracaena fragrans* 'Massangeana')

∞ English Ivy (*Hedera helix*)

∞ Variegated Snake Plant (*Sansevieria trifasciata* var. *laurentii*)

∞ Red-edged Dracaena (*Dracaena marginata*)

∞ Peace Lily (*Spathiphyllum* 'Mauna Loa')

∞ Florist's Chrysanthemum (*Chrysanthemum morifolium*)

>> And as a cook I can recommend a small *Aloe vera* in your kitchen—not only are they low-maintenance plants, but the sap has terrific healing properties if you burn yourself while cooking.

>> Once a week buy (or cut if you're fortunate enough to have a garden and they're in season) some fresh flowers. A small posy of flowers along with some votives is the simplest starting point for creating hygge in the home. Stick to one variety of flower or one shade, and resist the urge to buy mixed bunches—they just look twee.

>> Shades of viridian, blue, grey and natural slate/blonde are intrinsically soothing and provide the right backdrop for your stylish Nordic (-inspired) furnishings. It doesn't take much to create hygge, wherever you are.

# two

—

# outdoor
# pursuits

# The Lure of
the Outdoors

**'It is better to go skiing and think of God,
than go to church and think of sport.'**

Fridtjof Nansen

By now you will have gathered that we Nordics are really in our element when outdoors. But, more importantly, for us, to be active at all times of the year is to be *alive*. So life takes place as much outdoors as indoors in our little corner of the world. And as Norwegian explorer Fridtjof Nansen once suggested: pondering God, the meaning of life, or just the bigger picture, is best done while *doing* something active in nature

## The Outdoors is Always Preferable to the Gym

If you have a choice, then opting for *friluftsliv* over a workout in the gym is a good start in your quest for true Nordic hygge. Compared to exercising indoors, multiple studies have shown that we reap substantial benefits when we slip into our exercise gear and get sweaty in nature. As we touched on in the previous chapter, time spent outdoors can improve your mental health and reduce stress levels but a workout in the wild rather than the gym also leads to a surge in energy levels, decreased anger and a healthy dose of vitamin D. You flex your brain in a positive way when flexing your muscles outdoors. Science seems to have confirmed what we intuitively knew, which is neatly encapsulated in this Norwegian expression:

*Ut på tur, aldri sur!* (Out on a hike, never grumpy!)

So outdoorsiness is deeply embedded in the Nordic DNA. Perhaps it's a legacy of the Vikings—that restless urge to be active, to go on adventures, to explore the world—it really is integral to our sense of who we are. Of course, there are public health issues in the region that echo those found in other developed societies—the blight of cancer, heart disease, a rise in obesity and other serious illnesses—but they are found in a smaller percentage of the Nordic population as a whole compared to neighbouring countries. In every scientifically accepted index measuring public health and longevity, the Nordic countries consistently top the list. It seems to me that the invigorating effects of fresh air, combined with time spent in nature in quiet contemplation and a sensible approach to life, means people in the region have got most of their priorities right.

And now that more of us are city dwellers than at any previous time in history, the Nordic example of outdoor living is instructive in how to manage your life and make the most of your time on this planet. So let's delve into the world of Nordic outdoor hygge …

# 'Hatar Sport! Hatar Sport!'

In Lukas Moodysson's critically acclaimed film *We Are the Best!*, set in 1980s Stockholm, a trio of teenage girls rebel against the status quo by forming a punk band. 'Hate sport! Hate sport!' they bellow while clanging at drums and a bass guitar with about as much musical finesse as Animal from *The Muppet Show*. The song—and I use the term loosely—is their protest against the tyranny of PE lessons after their encounter with a disagreeable teacher. He treats their lack of interest in team sports with contempt and as a punishment makes the girls run laps around the gym. 'The world is a morgue but you're watching Bjorn Borg!' they sing in response to the teacher's boorishness, and the lyrics are particularly amusing to anyone who grew up in as sports-mad a region as ours. It's a cliché that sport is now regarded as a global religion; well, in the Nordic region it's *definitely* in the realm of the sacred.

Some of you reading this book will be able to relate to those girls and their rejection of school PE lessons. Perhaps you too were put off sports for life thanks to a PE-related trauma in your youth. When I was a pupil at the British International School in Oslo we had a British PE teacher in primary school who believed that girls should only take part in netball, rounders and callisthenics. The boys were allowed to do whatever they wanted and I took umbrage at the unfairness that they were able to play football when we had no choice but to play

∞
Getting kids outdoors as early as possible is the Nordic philosophy

netball, or contort ourselves into odd tree shapes. Our teacher's decidedly Victorian attitude to gender and sport was completely out of step with the Norwegian approach—girls can play whatever game they want and no one accuses them of being unfeminine, or worries about their wombs dropping out, or any of the other nonsense spouted by chauvinists to exclude girls and women from the world of sport.

In many countries, this archaic attitude to girls taking part in sport still exists. At precisely the time when sport can help alleviate the stresses of school and the angst of being a teen, so many girls are put off physical exercise and team sports for life. That's why the Swedish government's initiative to encourage girls and women to participate in sport is an enlightened policy: nationally, 40 per cent of all those who do some kind of sport in Sweden are female. The emphasis is on finding a sport that you enjoy and to build confidence, not to incubate the next Olympic

—————— *"The mountain calls you when there's a fresh layer of crisp white snow."*

champion. The government recognizes that investing in these initiatives has significant social and economic benefits—not only are people happier when they've taken part in a sport they find fun, but the habits they develop at a young age will stay with them for life, meaning increased longevity and fewer lifestyle-related illnesses to treat within the Swedish health system. Why wouldn't we want girls and women to take part in such a scheme? It's absurd that in many parts of the world half the population is systematically discouraged either from finding a sport they love or from being outdoorsy.

If you're reading this and you're no longer in the first flush of youth, you've been put off sports for life and you fear taking up a new activity when you're no longer a sprightly teen, then take heart: a recent study in the US found that even if you've come to sport and physical activity later in life after a prolonged sedentary period, you still improve your chance of living longer and gain the manifold benefits to your mental health, so it's *never* too late to start.

As Anna Kessel writes in her book *Eat Sweat Play*, it's high time women reclaimed sport as something fun to do. It doesn't have to be a chore, or humiliating. You don't have to come first or leave everyone else in your wake. Yes, competition can be exhilarating, and as humans we have evolved to go further, faster and to be stronger with each generation, but sport teaches you so much more about how to live your life. Sport doesn't have to be brutal and fierce; it can be gentle and relaxed, and it's only really as adults that we fully realize the upside of a sporting life: that team spirit and solidarity learnt on a playing field can help you in your career; that being physically active means you exude confidence; you walk taller, look strangers in the eye and apply the lessons of real sportsmanship to other aspects of your life. It's a real pity that so many people abandon sport after they leave higher education, and resort to the gym as a means of staying fit. Don't get me wrong—it's always better to do some activity even if it's indoors on a treadmill, but there's not much joy to be found in gyms. A University of Cambridge study found that inactivity was far more dangerous to our health than being overweight, with a higher rate of morbidity among those who are sedentary compared to those who are obese, confirming the suspicion long held by many of us who are active that it doesn't matter what body shape you are, or how high or low your BMI is—the key to longevity is to be *active*.

In the Nordic region, sport isn't viewed as a zero-sum game that's all about winning. Everything from the usual winter suspects—skiing, skating, hockey and ski-jumping—to football during the more clement months,

handball, athletics, rowing, sailing … all sports are big news, and people get excited about their athletes doing well in international championships, but it's hardly a national tragedy if your side loses. You might feel a little sad if your team crashes out of a big competition but then you get yourself outdoors and forget about it. At the Lillehammer Winter Olympics in 1994, the Norwegian cross-country relay team were hot favourites to win their race, one of the most eagerly anticipated events for Nordic skiing enthusiasts. When Italy won instead, the decidedly partisan audience of local Norwegians was stunned, but it wasn't considered the end of the world. Contrast that with the way the British press builds up expectations about England at every major football championship and then gleefully shreds the team and their manager when they fail to win.

—— *"To understand Nordic hygge is also to look at the traditions we carry on today that shape and define us."*

It's not all about traditional sports, however. Cast a glance at the more unusual Nordic outdoor pursuits such as Finland's *eukonkanto*, a race in which men carry their wives through an obstacle course. Much like England's tradition of cheese-rolling on Cooper's Hill in Gloucestershire, Finnish wife-carrying races are wonderfully bonkers, but that's precisely the point—sport *can* be silly; it's about not taking yourself too seriously. In a world in which professional sports have become so heavily commercialized, we forget how much fun can be found in unglamorous outdoor activities …

# Hunting & Fishing

*'Fishing relaxes me. It's like yoga, except I still get to kill something.'*
—                                                (Ron Swanson, *Parks and Recreation*)

Much has been made of the Nordic love of foraging, an activity popularized by chefs such as René Redzepi of Copenhagen's most famous restaurant, Noma, but less focus has been directed at our hunting and fishing traditions. Frankly, it's impossible to have a discussion about Nordic outdoor activities without touching on what some may find a sensitive subject. Let me be clear: fishing and hunting are a way of life in the region. They are not associated with class or wealth, but simply activities that have been practised throughout our history as a means of survival. We Nordics have a pragmatic approach to hunting and fishing. For many, these are traditions central to our identity, and responsible hunters and fishermen (and women) practise them with the utmost respect for animals and abide by the rules established by governments. Historically, any property with hunting and fishing rights was regarded as extremely valuable, and our family had such a farm. I grew up among relatives who fished trout in the nearby streams during summer and hunted birds and deer in the autumn.

I asked Sara Malm, a Swedish hunter and foreign news reporter at MailOnline, about the subject. She confirmed that in Sweden too hunting is seen as a way of life, not associated with any particular background but rather practised in families who are predominantly from rural areas. Like me, Sara was raised with an assortment of animals, such as deer, moose, boar and hares, hanging in a garage (in our family's case it was a nearby hut on the farm). Hunting for Sara is 'about the whole experience rather than the moment I fire a gun. I get to spend time in nature, at peace, far away

∞
Preserving food, such as smoking fish, stems from a need to have sufficient supplies to see us through the long winter months

35

from London life ... hunting can sometimes be one long waiting game, and I can be sat at my stand for hours without seeing a single animal and be happy with that.'

Echoing Ron Swanson's comment above, Sara likens hunting to yoga but with a shotgun. The meditative calm that comes from hunting and fishing is a frequently cited reason for taking part in this activity, but Sara also told me there is a profound moral reason for her decision to follow in her father's footsteps and seek her hunting licence: 'I am also a big meat eater, and I believe that as such you've got to take responsibility for your diet. By hunting, I can—in essence—follow the meat from birth to plate. I know the meat is healthy, has had a happier life than much of the meat available in a supermarket, and it's better for the environment and minimizes waste. I also think it's important to face the fact that in order for me to eat meat, an animal has to die. It may sound like "no shit Sherlock" but a lot of people are happy to buy crap bacon from a supermarket, but are horrified when they see videos from slaughterhouses and have to face the consequences of buying cheap products.' If you're a meat eater and squeamish about the idea of killing animals then Sara's words may make you uncomfortable, but she is right: this quintessentially Nordic outdoor pursuit is not merely a sport; it is about respecting nature and about owning the fact that eating an animal is a deeply moral act. Perhaps it's odd to include this subject under the rubric of hygge, but I don't see any point in sugar-coating the reality: to understand Nordic hygge and the way we live is also to look at the traditions we carry on today that shape and define us.

# Skiing is a Dance & the Mountain Always Leads

Naturally, skiing reigns supreme in the Nordic region. Everything from traditional cross-country, to downhill, to freestyle jumps and moguls, snowboarding, classic Telemark and the frankly terrifying genre of ski-jumping. We're not *quite* born with skis as the saying goes, but we start very, very young. As someone who grew up with an ace skier for a father I was enrolled at the age of four in our local Oslo ski school, run by local skiing legend Tomm Murstad. Even in the 1990s, when he was well into his twilight years, you would see old Tomm whizzing around the neighbourhood on cross-country skis. We believe that skiing truly is for life, there's simply no excuse to be slothful—no matter how old you are, those skis are to be used whenever the conditions are right. The mountain calls you when there's a fresh layer of crisp white snow on the ground.

I was lucky to learn how to cross-country and downhill ski at a young age, and my parents were always encouraging. As you can see in photos in this book, skiing was a family affair and there were times when I'd fall over and almost give up, but that was OK. I'd just brush myself down and get up, keep going. Usually with the promise of a bun or a hot chocolate—nothing builds resilience quite like the promise of baked treats and a chocolatey drink! Then one day I saw my best childhood friend crash into a tree and smash his face and it was game over on the downhill skiing front. The fear set in and I haven't been down a steep slope since the late 1980s, a source of considerable consternation to my parents—they couldn't figure out why, without any explanation, I suddenly quit. The truth is I was too embarrassed to admit how scared I was, it felt like I'd failed in some way, that I was less Norwegian for it. A point-blank refusal to go downhill skiing and that was that. It wasn't until many years later that I told them why and all was forgiven. I hadn't failed, of course; it was just an early sign that I wasn't going to develop into a thrill-seeking teenager, and later a reckless adult. Caution was imprinted from that point onwards, and it took a long time for me to *own* it.

But looking back I wonder why I should ever have felt ashamed for not wanting to do something. You're not going to fully grasp outdoor hygge if all you do is push yourself to extreme limits; you have to discover what you enjoy and not worry about the activities that aren't meant for you. After all, who cares if you're not into a particular sport? The key is to find what makes you happy, and for me that's the rigour and elegance of cross-country skiing over downhill. Some downhill skiers insist that cross-country is boring and looks too much like hard work—so what? I don't judge them for their desire to crash down a mountain like a maniac. Each to their own.

# Focus on What Your Body Can Do ...

'Everyone looks so healthy'—it's an observation I've heard time and again from friends and colleagues who visit the Nordic region, to which I usually reply that it's thanks to our love of butter. Joking aside, arguably this has something to do with the Nordic approach to the human body. One of the

*"For us, to be active at all times of the year is to be alive."* ———

clichés about the Nordic countries is that we're quite open about our bodies; we like to go buck-naked in a sauna, some of us really go in for naturism, and public nudity is no big deal. To some extent that is true—we are, by and large, really comfortable in our birthday suits. As always, there's more to our love of nudity than meets the eye. I didn't give it much thought until after spending my gap year in Japan, where they have a similarly relaxed approach to the body. If you've ever been to a Japanese hot spring you'll know what I mean. Everyone's in the nude and it's nothing special. They also have a culture of impeccable hygiene, which is something Nordics can relate to. We're obsessed with cleanliness, a subject I'll touch on later.

At any rate, I arrived in the UK after that experience abroad to study at university and discovered that attitudes to the body were rather more … problematic. Shame and embarrassment about what the body does (poop and periods, for example) and how it *looks* seem to be a much greater preoccupation here than what I encountered growing up in Norway, where boobs and bums were nothing special. They were just *there*. Thighs weren't something you had to whittle down to matchsticks but useful parts of our bodies for skiing, kicking a football and hiking.

My theory, formulated over a whisky (or two), is that in a region marked by long, harsh winters you were judged for what you could do. In other words, survival was the aim when it was winter eight months of the year, and a skinny so-and-so wasn't much use if he or she didn't possess the strength to shovel metres of snow away from a cabin, carry wood or fend off a bear. The elements will test you in unexpected ways, and a strong body is one that stands the most chance of survival. If you've ever watched an episode of the History channel's *Vikings* then you'll have noticed that Viking women fought alongside the men, and took part in raids as shield maidens and equally fierce warriors as the men. Archaeological evidence confirms this, with recent finds suggesting that women fought alongside their warrior brethren and were buried with the same honours.

I was reminded of this when I came across the world CrossFit champion Annie Thorisdottir (Icelandic for 'Thor's Daughter'—a fitting name for Annie) in an issue of US *Vogue* a few years back. Named the 'fittest woman on the planet', Annie's strength and ability is exceptional, yes, but also instructive. She is fierce, she is determined and she is completely at ease with her immense strength. In the *Vogue* interview, she stated her desire to inspire women and young girls to 'focus more on what their bodies can do, than on how they look', and this is really the Nordic outdoor hygge philosophy in a nutshell. If you spend your life only pursuing activities to hone your body so it *looks* good, or with the sole purpose of being as skinny as possible, you have completely missed the point. A preoccupation with how your body looks is a certain path to low self-esteem and anxiety, a finding that is backed up by numerous studies on body image and mental health. Skiing, playing football, kayaking, running outdoors, swimming— first and foremost, these activities allow you to feel great, with the added benefit that they build strong bodies. If you happen to look all right too then that's a nice bonus, but it's decidedly not the end goal.

∞

Papa Johansen, an ace ski instructor in his day, taught me to ski before I was even out of nappies

# Free the Body, Free the Mind

Any time you hit a low remember Annie's wise words, and ask what your body can do. Think about the last time you were really in awe of your body.

I mean it! Don't be bashful. Our bodies are marvels of biology, chemistry and physics, designed to keep us in a finely calibrated state of homeostasis—often it's not until we're sick that we fully appreciate what our bodies can do. All those products you read about, or see in the 'health' section of a store, promising a detox? Your liver, kidneys and extended digestive system all do an excellent job of flushing out any detritus for you. It's estimated that the global fitness and wellbeing industry in 2017 will be worth a staggering $1 trillion. That's right, one *trillion* dollars. A 'health' industry by and large predicated on making you feel bad about yourself—how perverse is that? Instead of being seduced by faddy diets and wasting money on expensive supplements with little or no clinical evidence to back up the claims of everlasting health, pare everything back and change your attitude. Free your body; be proud and grateful for what it can do and ignore all that nonsense. After all, 'ideal' body types are simply part of a toxic narrative that is totally un-hygge. Resist that narrative and you will feel so much better for it. Too many people—especially women—are socially conditioned to hate their bodies. So instead train yourself to channel your inner Queen Lagertha from *Vikings*. By that I don't mean crack someone's skull in half with an axe when they make a snide remark about your body, but give them your most imperious stare and walk away. The next time you see an advertisement designed to make you feel bad about yourself, or if you hear someone criticizing another person for their body shape, ask 'Who cares?' Even just the act of saying it feels liberating. Free yourself of any negative thoughts about your body and free your mind.

# Find What Works Best for You

Face it, we all know that life as a sloth would be the easy option, and we humans have a knack for inventing things that make us go further, faster and higher. While we're grateful for the cars, trains, airplanes and space shuttles that have revolutionized our lives, we're also getting more sedentary, and the battle against obesity in developed countries is now almost a daily feature of news bulletins. The fact of the matter is, technology allows us to do great things and can open our minds in ways our ancestors could never have imagined, but it also gives us the excuse to not be as physically active as we could, and should, be.

∞

If you want to invest in your health and fitness, a bicycle is probably a better start than a gym membership

Much like the saying that you should trust a busy person to get a job done, it's a truth that being active begets more energy, and being slothful means you're more likely to remain a couch potato. Whether that's because as humans we're creatures of habit, or because of some quirk in our evolutionary hard-wiring, who knows? Living in a city like London means I can be super-lazy if I wish, or the city can spur me on in unexpected ways.

Yes, modern urban living requires that you make certain compromises when it comes to outdoor pursuits, that much is obvious. As much as I'd love to spend every spare hour picking lilies of the valley and going for leisurely, meditative hikes in a nearby empty forest, there are certain mitigating circumstances to consider: central London's high levels of air pollution for starters—a recent report found that the city's poor air quality was not only damaging to the respiratory system, but also has a pronounced effect on our skin, leading to premature ageing—proximity (or lack thereof) of

*"Time spent outdoors can improve your mental health and reduce stress levels."* —————

locations where I can safely spend time outdoors after dark; the Thames being a somewhat less than ideal swimming pool to splash around in. During winter I can't just clip on my cross-country skis and go for a spin around Bloomsbury's squares at the end of a long day. There are plenty of swanky gyms and fitness studios nearby, but the smugness of the kale and overpriced Lycra crowd just makes me want to punch a wall. Besides, a recent study found that indoor gym equipment is riddled with as much undesirable bacteria as the inside of a toilet bowl. Spritzing yourself with antiseptic spray every time you hit the weights? No thanks.

Here's my outdoor hygge philosophy: I get outdoors whenever possible, and make compromises about fitness when I'm in the city. It really helps to think of your outdoor activity portfolio as you would your stock portfolio and diversify. That might mean twenty minutes of yoga in your nearest park or outdoor square first thing in the morning, and walking around the centre of the city whenever possible, avoiding busy main roads to steer clear of too much air pollution. Long walks on Hampstead Heath, or along the river on a sunny weekend. In winter, the music at my local BOOM Cycle studio in Holborn makes a workout feel like a party and the endorphin rush from a cardio session is just the tonic when you're feeling stressed or the city's grinding you down. Aside from being immensely fun, spin cycling has also helped me to rediscover the joy of cycling outdoors again after a hiatus (London traffic is terrifying, so I stay on quieter side streets). Like many of you reading this, part of my travel preparations include scouting the fitness options before departing and invariably packing a swimsuit and/ or a pair of trainers or hiking boots, along with a basic workout kit. Press trips in the past have introduced the joy of kayaking (in Cork, Ireland) and the thrill of husky sledding (near Røros, Norway), and I daydream about new activities to try: archery, jujitsu, canoeing, mountain climbing, a Tough Mudder challenge ... gentle pursuits, that kind of thing.

Perhaps you're rolling your eyes at all this. I mean, how many hours in the day can you possibly devote to outdoor pursuits? Full disclosure: I haven't always been diligent in staying active. Yet after I wrote my first two cookbooks on Scandinavian food, I was always tired, my clothes didn't fit terribly well and I was crabby. Why? Well, all that recipe-testing during a short period (alongside work on twelve other cookbooks), coupled with a prolonged lethargic spell due to illness, meant those cinnamon buns had to go somewhere. If I'd been a bear going into hibernation in the wilderness that would have been useful, but I was a thirtysomething woman and I just wasn't feeling like my optimal self.

So one day I decided enough was enough, and did what my Nordic background taught me would work best: I got outdoors again. Recalling what I'd done during those angst-ridden teen years, when every exam mattered for the chance to enter a decent university and the sky felt like it was falling down, I got outside, moved around and shed that stress. It's a simple, time-honoured formula, and it didn't require much more than a little gumption and appropriate clothing. Most importantly, it works. We all face challenges at various points in our lives and sometimes everything feels out of control—that's when you have to step back and *reset*.

When the cinnamon buns had become happily married to my carb-loving hips, and I was at a low ebb, I knew it was time to do something. I signed up for a session with Charlene Hutsebaut, a Canadian personal trainer specializing in biomechanics and a positive approach to health and fitness. She sent over a lengthy questionnaire for me to fill in, about my personal health, family history, lifestyle, what sort of work I did (and how sedentary I was); about my diet and eating habits, and correlated questions about mood. Just the act of filling in the form got me thinking about the more long-term goals I had in mind, and also what sort of regime might be sustainable. What's more, Charlene talked openly about how important it was not to become *fixated* on any specific fitness goals, but rather to savour the joy of new activities.

If you're stuck in a sedentary rut and can't quite decide what sort of activity will work for you, fret not. It may be tempting to jump on the latest celebrity-endorsed fitness bandwagon—but if you really want to experience the joy of Nordic living then you need to find a way to practise hygge outdoors and indoors that works for you.

For many people running is invigorating and life-affirming; in fact, one of my favourite books written on sport is Alexandra Heminsley's *Running Like a Girl*. I love the simplicity of running: all you need is a pair of decent trainers and a little motivation. Unfortunately, I happen to run like a demented and very angry penguin so it's not for me, but I can swim for hours without feeling tired or bored. Therefore, I decided to join our local YMCA to swim three times a week, alternating these sessions with yoga classes. Non-swimmers like to point out how dull swimming is, all those lengths up and down a pool, but as Leanne Shapton observes in her book *Swimming Studies*:

*'As I swim, my mind wanders. I talk to myself. What I can see through my goggles is boring and foggy, the same view lap by lap. Mundane,*

*unrelated memories flash up vividly and randomly, a slide show of shuffling thoughts. They flash up and fade, like the thoughts that float peripherally before sleep, either inconsequential or gathering momentum into anxiety before eventually dissolving.'*

Shapton's words will undoubtedly resonate with swimmers, but runners I speak to also talk of the 'zone' they get into when they head outdoors for a jog. The mind becomes a 'slide show of shuffling thoughts'—it's precisely what happens when you find the right form of exercise for your body type and temperament.

Whenever I get out of London and am near a coastline I go for a dip in the sea and experience what Damon Young, in his book *How to Think about Exercise*, calls the 'joyful fear' of wild swimming, a fear that I find exhilarating rather than terrifying, unlike when I think of downhill skiing. It's that peculiar drive when you find the right outdoor activity for you: fear becomes something you can embrace, and that has a way of percolating through to everyday life.

'Effort is a choice' says a motivational billboard at my local YMCA. Anthropologists like to talk about 'agency' and how, as social agents, we humans exercise that agency, so in the case of fitness and outdoor pursuits here's the *How to Hygge* philosophy: You choose to be active, you choose to go outside, you choose to make the most of your body.

Effort really is a choice, and the human body is capable of an extraordinary range of activities, so why wouldn't you want to be as active as physically possible?

# The *How to Hygge* Outdoor Philosophy in a Nutshell

∞  To be active is to be alive.

∞  The outdoors is always preferable to the gym.

∞  Don't punish yourself if you can't get outdoors whenever you want. Make smart compromises that work for you.

∞  Take up a sport, even if it's as a bystander or supporter of a club. Find the fun in sport.

∞  If you experienced a PE-related trauma in your childhood, please don't let that deter you from taking up an activity later in life.

∞ Being clumsy, falling over, narrowly avoiding trees when skiing, having little hand-to-eye coordination ... none of it matters. Looking like a dork when exercising is absolutely fine. So what if you're a klutz? I am and it hasn't stopped me being the most physically active now than at any previous time in my life.

∞ Even if your body is clumsy, it's still a magnificent feat of engineering. Marvel at what your body can do.

∞ If you've had a sedentary period and feel daunted by the prospect of being active, start with baby steps. Good habits take time to develop, but studies show that even making one small change to your everyday routine can make all the difference. A twenty-minute walk in a local park will lift your spirits and clear your head whatever time of the year it is.

∞ Diversify that activity portfolio. Doing the same thing over and over is going to mean you plateau pretty fast and you'll get stuck in a rut. Try new activities whenever you can.

∞ Throw away those weighing scales. Concentrate on how being active makes you feel, how your energy levels soar, how much better your posture is ... everything else is a bonus. If you focus solely on how you look, you'll never really be happy.

∞ If you run like a demented penguin and find it truly awful then it's OK to resist the pressure to take up this most revered of activities. I only like running when playing football and even then I only like sprints. Running enthusiasts will try to convert you, but if your gut is telling you no, then listen to your gut. Find something that you enjoy.

∞ It's never too late to join a team, and if there isn't one then band together with like-minded friends and form your own. Give something back by coaching the next generation if you have the time and inclination.

∞ Don't be too hard on yourself; sometimes a gentle walk just taking in the scenery is enough.

∞ No one ever regrets being active outdoors, especially if there's a delicious reward at the end of it ...

# three

## the spirit of
## self-sufficiency

# Hygge Life Skills

'Self-sufficiency is the greatest of all wealth.'

Epicurus

It's safe to say that living a Nordic life to its fullest means being as active as possible, at every age. The call of the wild inspires us to enjoy hygge outdoors as much as we do indoors, so whether it's going for long hikes in the mountains and forests, spending an afternoon gardening, or just heading to a local park to climb a tree, the main thing is to find joy in simple activities all year round. Perhaps you've been motivated by the awesome athleticism of the Olympics or Paralympics to establish your own team for a weekly dose of sporting camaraderie—whatever activity you choose will add to your quality of life so much more than spending your free time in idleness.

It seems to me that there is another aspect of the Nordic love of being active which remains under-explored: our spirit of self-sufficiency. To be human is to be active, that much is clear. But knowing how to do and make things is also vital to our sense of who we are, something that's often forgotten in our digital age. Indeed, the ability to carry out a variety of tasks is deeply embedded in our DNA. As Yuval Noah Harari observes in *Sapiens: A Brief History of Humankind*, our ancestors foraged for food and materials, but also for knowledge:

*'To survive they needed a detailed mental map of their territory. To maximise the efficiency of their daily search for food, they required information about the growth patterns of each plant and the habits of each animal. They needed to know which foods were nourishing, which made you sick, and how to use others as cures.*

From what the archaeological record tells us early *sapiens* didn't just haphazardly gain knowledge for the fun of it. They developed essential skills out of necessity, and honed them so they could survive:

'*Each individual had to understand how to make a stone knife, how to mend a torn cloak, how to lay a rabbit trap, and how to face avalanches, snakebites or hungry lions. Mastery of each of these many skills required years of apprenticeship and practice.*'

Harari suggests that most of us modern *sapiens* would struggle to turn a flint stone into a spear with the speed and precision that an early forager could. I certainly wouldn't know how to do so unless I was taught by an expert and dedicated myself to hours of study and practice, no doubt sustaining a few injuries along the way. Archaeologists constantly uncover evidence of skills in the kinds of objects found buried in graves and long-abandoned settlements—these objects were part of material cultures which help us understand how our ancestors lived. When my Norwegian great-grandfather found Viking-era artefacts buried on Skaim, his farm in Sogn and Fjordane, researchers identified objects as diverse as ornate jewellery, bronze clasps for clothing, intricately designed clay pots that had been made in Ireland, religious symbols and an array of objects that required a degree of knowledge, creativity and sophistication to design and make.

Early humans possessed the ability to scan the landscape for danger, to make things—often of great beauty—to protect themselves, to survive in hostile conditions and therefore to propagate the species: these skills have been at the core of human existence for the better part of our history.

Aside from the cosy act of propagating the species, ask yourself if you would really know what to do in the face of the sorts of challenges our ancestors faced. Without the training acquired by an apothecary or in the field of botany, it's unlikely most of us would be able to discern which plants offer potential cures for ailments and illness. Yet historically that traditional knowledge was gathered through experience (and no doubt a fair amount of trial and error—we figured out early on to be wary of bitter plants as they might be poisonous) and passed on down the generations until it became embodied knowledge.

I was reminded of this on a midsummer hike through the Aurlandsdalen, or the Aurland valley, a nineteen-kilometre trek through beautiful scenery in western Norway. Between the waterfalls cascading down along our route and the quaint little *hytte* (cabins) speckled remotely across steep cliffs, what struck me during our hike was the diversity of plants and flowers growing in abundance: everything from small, wild orchids to strawberries, blueberries, cloudberries, lilies of the valley, the highly poisonous wolf's bane, any number of small, cheerful mountain flowers and lush, primordial ferns, everywhere. Accompanying us on our hike, my cousin Anne Christine explained many of the plants' names and what their function was— information she'd picked up from her elders. That kind of knowledge is essential if you're studying botany and horticulture, but for anyone who isn't taught what those plants mean and what they can do for us, they simply look pretty. It seems a shame to go through life without some insight into what grows around us, or understanding of our landscape, but then I conform to the twenty-first-century cliché that 'plant lady is the new cat lady' thanks to a mild obsession with plants and flowers!

As for food, well we're still debating what it truly means to be healthy which foods nourish us the best, and although modern science has allowed us to understand the minutiae of nutrition, for many people knowing which foods are going to optimize their health and longevity remains a mystery. Witness the endless media coverage of the latest fad diet, or the scientific endeavours trying to establish whether we should be eating more carbs or more fat. Hence the appeal for many of eating locally grown, seasonal produce—that simple philosophy cuts through a lot of the confusing messages we hear about food and health.

Nowadays in order to survive we no longer need a wide and deep pool of knowledge or skills to draw on. Thanks to modern amenities and the way our societies function one could argue that we modern *sapiens* have become a little flabby, both physically and mentally. After all, why bother making an effort to learn an essential skill when we have so many ingenious gadgets and everything is accessible at the swipe of a smartphone? The absence of any real *need* to track down and hunt a deer to eat, or to know which plant might poison us, means we can rely on our local supermarket, or place orders online for pretty much anything we desire—and trust that what we put in our mouths won't kill us.

We are so dependent on other people doing or making things for us that we rarely give the matter any thought; most of us have become detached from the manufacturing process. And no doubt our modern-day reliance on technology, and ineptitude when it comes to doing things our ancestors had to master in order to survive, would lead to a certain amount of eye-rolling on their part. I fully confess my knowledge is patchy when it comes to household DIY and understanding how electrics and plumbing really work—though I can change a light bulb, have painted several rooms in my time and can read maps thanks to childhood orienteering lessons at winter ski camp. I have also inherited my family's predilection for scrubbing interiors until they look spotless, thereby conforming to the Nordic cliché that we're neat freaks, a theme I'll return to later on when it comes to design and home.

Useful skills undoubtedly, but more importantly within the context of hygge they also add an element of *contentedness* to my life. I like being able to do simple stuff that doesn't require another person to be hired in for a specific task. For me, a good quality of life requires a few basic skills so that I can exist in a state of self-sufficiency, rather than resorting to short-term, quick fixes to every problem. It's a long-term, sustainable strategy for living. At the very least it means I have a hygge home …

So one of the elements at the core of Nordic living is knowing how to do useful stuff. How to chop wood, make a decent fire, paint a room, even team up with a group of friends and build a cabin. Making a piece of furniture, or knitting a scarf—things we would have had to know how to do in another age if we wanted to sit at a table or stay warm in winter. The phenomenal success of recent books such as Lars Mytting's *Norwegian Wood: Chopping, Stacking and Drying Wood the Scandinavian Way* and Robert Penn's *The Man Who Made Things Out of Trees*, not to mention Norway's knitting kings Arne & Carlos, attests to a widespread craving for simplicity, a deep primal urge to make things with our hands, to connect with our natural environment again—harnessing a creative energy to good effect. The pleasure gained from making something, even if you don't have to, is tantalizing to those of us who have grown up not actually *needing* to do those things. Getting decent grades at school and finding a profession to pursue is all well and good, but in times of economic uncertainty, and a shift away from the 'jobs for life' culture that many of our parents and grandparents expected and worked hard for, means a new generation are turning to simpler pursuits that have meaning and value. Many of us may not be rich by conventional standards, but for those who have chosen a different path, our wealth really does lie in some form of self-sufficiency …

# Back to Basics

Across the Nordic region many people still choose to go foraging for berries and edible plants in the summer months, savouring the short autumnal season of wild mushrooms. It's obviously not out of necessity, and much has been made of the Nordic love of foraging to the point where New Nordic Food is now viewed by many as synonymous with foraged

food. What is sometimes omitted in the features written about this corner-stone of our food culture is that it's anchored in a culture of self-reliance, of preserving a heritage in the region that, until relatively recently in human history, had more in common with those foragers, hunters and gatherers thousands of years ago than present-day, technologically savvy *sapiens*. Plus it's fun. We get outdoors, pick some berries, gather a few wild flowers to take home, and stretch the legs. It's a gentle workout with a bonus!

The myth is that we all go foraging in the summer and autumn months, but that's not necessarily the case. It's simply not possible for us all to survive on foraged foods—there aren't enough berries and mushrooms in nature to feed everyone—so, much like our approach to staying active, we make compromises and buy most of our food from supermarkets. As mentioned in the previous chapter, many people still go hunting and fishing, and those activities are central to a Nordic way of life, but the food found in the wild *supplements* that available in stores. There are undoubtedly true outdoorsmen and women living in a state of near autarky, but they are the exception, not the norm.

The methods associated with traditional Nordic cooking have in recent years been revived by a new generation of chefs across the region, including for example how to salt cod, pickle berries, fruits and vegetables, bake bread, ferment dairy products, cure salmon, make berry cordials and, of course, how to ferment alcohol. That chimes with a wave of renewed interest in the ancient art of fermentation among food lovers and cooks in North America, Britain and continental Europe. People are discovering that not only do time-honoured techniques such as the ones listed above add delicious new flavours and textures to a cooking repertoire, but there is a body of research now dedicated to understanding how those fermented and preserved foods may improve human health. Plus, as anyone who has made their own yoghurt, baked a loaf of bread or cultivated a kombucha starter will tell you: it's immensely satisfying.

Throughout history, humans across all societies and landscapes adapted to their environments thanks to nimble thinking that allowed them to stay safe, to eat nutritious food by preserving valuable ingredi-ents in a time before refrigeration, and to make it through long winters or intensely hot summers. Thanks to ingenuity, probably a few accidents and sheer grit, humans have survived. We made it! Yet romanticizing the good old days is certainly not my intention here. Throughout much of human history, life was tough, at times brutal, and our snaggletoothed ancestors were unlikely to live much past their thirties. Until very recently in our evolutionary history, life on this planet for the vast majority could often be 'solitary, poor, nasty, brutish, and short', to borrow philosopher Thomas Hobbes's cheerful assessment, and truth be told it still is hard for a great many people in the world today. We have much to thank science, dentistry and vaccines for, but I also firmly believe that channeling the Nordic spirit of self-sufficiency and learning a few new skills even after we've finished higher education can be life-affirming and add to the proven hygge joys of cake, candles and beautiful interiors.

Although my pantry is full to the brim with useful staples like pickles, preserved mackerel and crispbread to see me through a few days of no electricity (or at least to make a delicious open sandwich in the midnight hour), it's hardly a stash that's going to keep our household going through weeks if we suddenly found ourselves in a state of emergency, or the electricity grid was hacked and we had no way to cook food on our stove. Early *sapiens'* knowledge of the surrounding environment is something very few of us would legitimately be able to claim we possess today—we simply don't *need* to know all these things, Harari suggests, because we rely on a collective pool of specialists who have been accumulating useful knowledge individually, therefore most of us will specialize in something early on in our lives and then stick with it, outsourcing all the other stuff to those with the requisite know-how.

So, in the Nordic spirit of self-sufficiency, I wondered what the genuinely useful life skills we could all benefit from would be? The internet is saturated with lists of the things every upstanding citizen should know, some arguably more useful than others. Rubbing walnuts on a piece of scratched wooden furniture to cover up any unsightly marks is a useful tip: a simple and cost-effective fix to a problem anyone with pets will be familiar with. Making kindling for a fire out of Doritos? Maybe not quite as crucial, depending on how well stocked your pantry is. There are always salted pretzels on standby in our pantry for snacking emergencies but I suspect their lower fat content may result in a less combustible kindling ...

Having thought about all of this, and been inspired by Nick Offerman's rallying cry that we seek pleasure in simple things like woodworking, outdoor activities or a good steak (from *Paddle Your Own Canoe: One Man's Fundamentals for Delicious Living*—a funny and warm book written by a very funny and wise man), I cast around and conducted a mini vox pop. I asked colleagues and friends what they considered to be the five essential life skills we should all know. Invariably, the management of finances and how to budget came up—smart advice in our economically precarious times. The ability to read a map, which chimes with Harari's observation that modern humans don't know much about their surroundings anymore. Plus these days we all have maps on our smartphones, and in relying on those plus GPS we're losing our ability to navigate our way around by observing landmarks, or particular trees, stones and other physical clues.

Empathy, patience, conscious listening, communicating well and learning/practising delayed gratification all make eminent sense in our wired times, when everything is available at the tap or swipe of a digital device. Courtesy towards other cultures, to which I would add that learning another language is crucial—although I'm biased, being a 'third-culture kid' with three nationalities (Norwegian, British and American, plus a sprinkling of about seventeen others). Understanding fitness and health was something a few mentioned, an affirmation of previous chapters in this book—learning to find the fun in outdoor activities and sport really is so fundamental to living a good life. On top of this I would add that a basic knowledge of how the human body works, and histology (how our cells work), would go a long way towards helping those easily seduced by the claims of health quacks and wellness gurus in resisting their cod science.

Simple hacks like how to sew a button back on a shirt, how to fix a running toilet, how to keep a clean house and manage a tidying routine (without it taking over your life), laundering clothes without ruining them, and continuing to *learn* after you leave school or college: all suggestions that chimed with the research I had conducted for this chapter. Perhaps not quite so obvious but no less useful for the propagation of the species include: how to flirt, how to dance, how to give a good back-rub. I'm reasonably confident I can do all those things without flailing too much, so at least the Johansen DNA has some chance of surviving into the next generation.

Having worked in the food industry for nearly a decade, I would of course argue that cooking is undeniably a life skill we can all benefit from. It also helps with that whole propagation of the species business—to cook for someone is to love them. In fact, Harvard biological anthropologist Richard Wrangham's book *Catching Fire: How Cooking Made Us Human* suggests that mastering the art of cooking over a fire was one of the most crucial steps in our evolution, allowing us to derive more energy from our food so we didn't have to spend all day ruminating plants like other animals. Freeing up that extra energy meant our brains could develop. So cooking really is a modern life skill—in fact, outsourcing the sort of useful skills that our ancestors would have possessed is a theme Michael Pollan explores to great effect in his book *Cooked*. Much like GPS and smartphone maps have rendered our ability to navigate using our instincts and common sense completely useless, the reliance on convenience and junk food is to my mind one of the major problems of food cultures across the developed world. Wresting back control and acquiring the essential skill of cooking a few nourishing dishes during the week—in between the odd takeaway, ready meal or visit to a restaurant, let's not be fanatics about cooking—is not only better for your bank balance, but you know exactly what goes into your food. We all have to eat, and the simple joy and satisfaction of making something from scratch, of learning skills that make us less reliant on others to do things for us, is an empowering act in itself.

# How to Think Like a Cook

*'No one is born a great cook, one learns by doing.'*

—                                                            Julia Child

As several of my correspondents cited cooking as a life skill, I've devoted a sizeable portion of this book to the joy of food and drink. Eating is easy, but cooking is both science and alchemy, which is what makes it so exciting—and also intimidating to anyone who has watched those competitive cooking programmes on TV. Having taught many cookery classes over the years, one pattern I noticed early on in my career was that those who were more comfortable and confident in the kitchen had learnt a few cooking techniques from someone in their family, a friend or a partner. Watching someone else cook and absorbing their knowledge through practice is invaluable experience, and I'll be the first to admit it's hard to achieve the same from reading a recipe book, even a great recipe book.

I learnt to cook traditional Norwegian dishes by watching my grandmother make them—I had to, as she never wrote anything down; everything she knew about cooking had been passed down from her mother. With the exception of baking recipes, when she would rely on a few scribbled notes, all her cooking knowledge was locked in her memory. So I knew what a cardamom dough should feel like—something novice bakers often struggle with when they make their first loaf of bread or buns. One baker memorably described a perfect bread dough as feeling like a woman's breast, but I defer to the late, great Laurie Colwin, who writes in her brilliant book *Home Cooking* that bread should have the 'springy, soft texture of a baby's bottom'.

At any rate, if you want to simplify your life and you don't know where to start in the kitchen, then as a preamble to the subsequent chapters in this book, here's my take on how to think like a cook. I was taught by my family that you don't have to be rich to eat well, and that food can be both delicious and nourishing at the same time. For us Johansens, true hygge lies in the simple pleasure of self-sufficiency in the kitchen ...

# Twenty Steps to Nordic Kitchen Hygge

1 >> Master at least five ways to cook with nature's original superfood: the egg. Gently boil (the operative word being 'gently'), scramble in butter, poach and fry or make into an omelette: all a great start. Eggs are the one food I can eat at breakfast, brunch, lunch, as an afternoon snack or at dinner. They win every time. Being able to make an omelette Arnold Bennett, Spanish tortilla, a soothing vanilla soufflé, crisp pistachio meringues and coddled eggs is a bonus, but not essential.

2 >> Taste and season as you go. Repeat. So many follow a recipe to a T in terms of salt and pepper, yet everyone has different levels of tolerance when it comes to seasoning and spices. I like my food quite highly seasoned, you may not. Whatever you do, use sea salt judiciously, and ignore the health fascists who say we should eliminate all salt from our diets. Bland food is a waste of time and energy, and a little sea salt goes a long way to elevating a dish from OK to WOW.

3 >> Bread: there's a reason why it's referred to as the staff of life, and why we 'break bread with someone' as an act of kinship. Take the time to make a simple loaf of bread. All you need is good flour, water, salt and yeast (or no yeast if you opt to make your own sourdough starter) and a little patience. If you have the time, budget and inclination, then there is a wonderful bread festival every September in Denmark at Skærtoft Mølle. That's a hygge holiday right there!

4 >> With that bread, or any decent bread you happen to have in your kitchen, turn a sandwich into something noble: most of the salad suggestions in this book can be reconfigured to make Nordic open sandwiches.

And we have a mild obsession with butter. Indeed, the Danes have an expression for how much butter should grace your slice of bread: *tandsmør*, or 'tooth butter', which tells you how thick the butter should be spread. The art of making a great sandwich is one of the most underrated kitchen skills.

5 >> Make a monthly batch of chicken stock. This doesn't have to be complicated: all you need is a few chicken carcasses—you can use leftovers from a roast or pick them up for a song at a local butcher's—a pot large enough to hold them in and water to cover the bones. That's it. Add aromatics such as peppercorns, garlic, ginger, bay leaves, parsley stalks, fennel stalks, carrots, onions, whatever you wish, but know that the bones are essentially all you need to make good homemade stock. Simmer for a few hours and then remove the bones before reducing to a gelatinous consistency (usually about one-third of the liquid from when you started reducing). My favourite thing to ramp up the flavour and consistency of the stock is to add a pile of roasted or barbecued chicken wings with their skins—they deepen the flavour and make a seriously gelatinous stock, plus they're a perfect snack to munch on while you're cooking. Freeze your homemade chicken stock in an ice tray to pop whenever you need a few stock cubes for a dish. For vegetable stock: use your favourite vegetables (onions with their skins on for extra colour, carrots, fennel, leeks, garlic, parsley stalks, etc.) and add Japanese kombu (a type of kelp) for umami. This last ingredient is essential to give your vegetable stock that extra flavour dimension, which comes naturally from the bones in a chicken stock.

6 >> Cook a large batch of meaty stew, bolognese or chilli con carne and freeze in individual portions. Batch-cooking is a lifeline for everyone, and I mean *everyone*. I don't care how old-fashioned it sounds, this is a godsend when you're cold, tired and would prefer to steer clear of overpriced takeaways or ready meals. I like to know what's in my food, so I choose not to outsource what I consider a kitchen staple to anyone else, and by the time you've done all the prep and the dish is cooking, it's hardly any extra effort to make twelve portions instead of four. You can then use the dish as a base for pies, to put in wraps or whatever you fancy.

7 >> Onions *always* take longer to cook than a recipe tells you. Thank you to author and journalist Damian Barr for reminding me of this. It's the bane of every cook's life: not only the crying that ensues when you slice an onion,

but the time they take to sweat properly without burning. My tip to prevent the latter: add a pinch of sea salt to the pan when cooking and keep the heat low. If you want to accelerate the caramelization of onions, add a pinch of bicarbonate of soda and cook over a medium heat.

8 >> Filleting a fish, handling raw meat and having a basic knowledge of which cuts of meat to cook what with. Rule number one: get to know your local fishmonger and butcher if you have one. Ask lots of questions. With meat, be aware that the fillet is the most tender cut of the carcass but the least interesting in terms of flavour, so why bother wasting your money on it. Cheap cuts of meat often require a little more thought and longer cooking, but they are worth the extra effort—you reap the benefits in added flavour and texture.

_____ *"Keep it simple, don't overcomplicate cooking."*

9 >> Music is great to listen to while cooking and having an impromptu kitchen disco is all well and good, until you drop a butcher's knife perilously close to your foot (as I have done). It's also led to a few near-tumbles and I may have set fire to a tea towel or two when shimmying around the kitchen. All I can say is: dance responsibly ...

10 >> Practise making one favourite dessert at least three times, or until you've nailed it. It's a great source of pride for a cook to have one failsafe dessert in their repertoire, knowing it will always be a crowd-pleaser. As an example: one of the most failsafe desserts I resort to is the almond and elderflower cake on page 78. Incidentally, if you're contemplating a dessert with sweet potato, avocado, chia seeds, or anything 'clean', then you've kind of missed the point of hygge, which is about enjoying delicious food, not fretting about whether it's healthy.

11 >> If you really loathe baking and can't face it then that's fine. Berries can always be relied upon as an alternative—just spritz them with a little lemon juice and sugar or elderflower cordial if they're tart, or flambé them in a little brandy, Grand Marnier and fresh orange juice for a boozy berry dessert. Everyone loves sorbet and/or ice cream so you can't go wrong with that combo. Keep it simple, don't overcomplicate cooking—if you don't enjoy baking, who cares?

12 >> All traditional food cultures have relied on preserving methods and fermentation to keep valuable foodstuffs from spoiling. Now science is recognizing the manifold health benefits of those foods so if you're feeling adventurous, try fermenting something. The best advice out there is from Sandor Ellix Katz; check him out—you'll be inspired, I promise.

13 >> Everything tastes better with butter.

14 >> Cooking impromptu dishes during the week when you're limited for time relies on keeping a well-stocked pantry.

My fridge and pantry essentials are:

∞

∞

∞

∞ If you don't enjoy baking, who cares? Berries can always be relied on as a base for a simple dessert

∞ garlic

∞ dried and tinned legumes

∞ some animal fat, e.g. chicken schmaltz, ibérico fat, butter (of course)

∞ a couple of oils to drizzle, e.g. olive and argan

∞ Spanish and Asian rice varieties

∞ pasta

∞ plain or Greek yoghurt

∞ my favourite spices

∞ Peter's Yard sourdough crispbread

∞ oats and homemade muesli

In the freezer, there's always a variety of frozen berries, a packet of garden peas, a loaf of sliced bread, homemade freezer jams, chicken stock, a few portions of bolognese, stew or chilli con carne. I also replenish weekly with a variety of fresh fruit, vegetables, dairy products and more perishable items, and that's about it. Due to the Johansen family love of baking, our baking pantry is quite well stocked, but in truth you don't need much more than a few good flours, eggs, butter or neutral vegetable oil, nuts of choice, spices, vanilla extract, cocoa powder, dark cooking chocolate and raising agents, e.g. dried yeast, or fresh if you can source it.

15 >>  If you really want to amplify your cooking, then keep a supply of umami-rich ingredients to add a burst of flavour to otherwise plain dishes. Good cooks keep the following on standby for all those fridge-foraging emergencies:

∞ preserved anchovies (Abba are best if you want that Nordic taste; Spanish and Italian are also excellent)

∞ soy sauce

∞ chilli sauce

∞ Parmesan cheese

∞ preserved tomatoes, olives, capers, cucumbers, onions

∞ pickled vegetables like sauerkraut, kimchi

∞ seafood—it wouldn't be a Nordic pantry without some preserved fish such as herring, mackerel, salmon, trout and shellfish ...

∞ dried mushrooms

∞ potatoes—both plain and sweet

∞ seaweed

∞ all meat

16 >> Keep a few vinegars in your pantry, including one basic, cheap one for cleaning/deodorizing purposes. A pan that has a whiff of cooked fish, a spicy stew, something garlicky: all odours will disappear if you wash it in a vinegar solution. Vinegar is brilliant for giving glassware extra shine and, mixed with bicarbonate of soda, it will descale your kettle, too.

17 >> We eat as much with our eyes as our other senses, as evinced by how popular food photography is on Instagram and other social media. Cooks who like their food to look beautiful always do the following: display everything in odd numbers—three, five, seven, etc. Adding height to a dish will make it more appealing, as will keeping the tableware simple—no fussy patterns to distract from the food. Even the most beige plate of food looks perkier with the addition of a colourful relish and some fresh herbs or pickles.

18 >> The law of diminishing returns applies to every dish: the first few bites of a delicious dessert are always the most intense, but if you serve enormous portions of everything you're not increasing the pleasure of that food, merely stuffing the gullet and invariably leading to some digestive discomfort. Think of small handfuls of food rather than giant mounds the size of someone's head. Hours of indigestion after a feast is not very hygge at all ...

19 >> When shopping for food, always make a list and if you're on a budget prioritize spending your hard-earned money on valuable proteins such as eggs, preserved fish and energy-giving legumes and beans, seasonal greens and fruits in two or three different colours so that you get a balance of flavours and nutrients. Oats are a frugal staple and rightly so. You don't have to spend an obscene amount of money to eat and live well.

20 >> The greatest gift you can give as a cook (other than feeding your friends, and loved ones) is to pass on your skills to the next genera-tion, or indeed to someone who hasn't had the good fortune to learn how to cook. If you have the time and inclination, getting children involved in the kitchen is an act of hygge generosity—they love getting stuck in, seeing the alchemy of food at work and of course eating the fruits of their labour. Cooking is about caring, and that means sharing your knowledge too.

Now that we've covered the basics, I hope the next chapters on Nordic food and drink will inspire you even further ...

four
—
the joy
of fika

# Fika for All

What is the point of being active all year round if you can't also get together with your colleagues, friends or loved ones over a coffee and a slice of something sweet? That's the essence of 'fika'—a Swedish tradition akin to the German idea of *'Kaffee und Kuchen'*.

We love our carbs, especially during the long winter months when we need a little extra energy. After a vigorous dash down the ski slopes or a busy day at work, the satisfaction that comes from sinking your teeth into a freshly baked cardamom twist is hard to beat. But Nordic baking isn't about cramming as much sugar into cakes and sweets as possible. We regard sweetness as one of the characteristics of good baking, in harmony with the other key players such as grains, almonds, spices and seasonal fruit.

For us, it's important to enjoy these moments of everyday indulgence. As Anna Brones and Johanna Kindvall write in their excellent book *Fika: The Art of the Swedish Coffee Break*, to ask *'Ska vi fika?'* (Should we fika?) is not just about eating cake and drinking coffee, it's about slowing down, recalibrating. 'Fika is the time when everything else is put on hold.'

Across Sweden, workers in many companies gather each day to enjoy a fika moment. This daily act is what social scientists at Uppsala University call 'collective restoration' and studies have shown significant benefits to both business (happy employees make better employees) and to social bonding.

Fika is, therefore, a prime example of a balanced, Nordic philosophy of life: work efficiently, be active, eat what you love, and make the most of those convivial moments of downtime during the day. That is the essence of hygge, too. There's something for everyone in these recipes; some are easy to prepare, such as the Malty Banana Chocolate Chip Walnut Muffins, and others, like the Cardamom Doughnuts with Orange Blossom Honey, require a patient, more meditative approach. A celebratory fika is best embodied in the Sour Cherry Bundt Cake and the Sticky Ginger Cake with a Clementine Glaze, the latter given an extra festive twist with the addition of crimson pomegranate seeds. I also include several chocolate recipes as a nod to the fact that we Nordics are chocoholics. Please do seek out the best cocoa powder and cooking chocolate you can afford—you'll reap the benefits when baking.

# Cardamom Twists

Makes 25–30 twists

**Quintessentially Nordic, spiced twists and rolls are about as emblematic of our baking heritage as it gets. I've baked so many variations over the years but I always come back to this recipe. The key is to add ground cardamom to an enriched yeast dough. It's the same principle as adding vanilla to any muffin, cake or torte recipe—the flavour is so enhanced, why wouldn't you add it?**

*For the Dough*

1kg refined spelt flour

50g fresh yeast

150g golden caster sugar

550ml whole milk

100g butter

1½ tsp sea salt

1 tbsp freshly ground cardamom
   (or more if you like)

2 medium eggs, plus extra for the egg wash

vegetable oil, for the bowl

*For the Filling*

150g soft butter

150g golden caster sugar
   (or use half light brown muscovado
   sugar if you like a deeper flavour)

2 tsp freshly ground cardamom

1 tsp vanilla extract

*To Decorate (optional)*

flaked almonds

Swedish pearl sugar or demerara sugar

*Sieve* the flour into a large mixing bowl. Crumble the fresh yeast into the flour until it's fine and feels completely coated in flour. Add the sugar and stir through.

Next, heat the milk, butter, salt and cardamom until scalding and then set aside in a cold place so that the milk cools to below 50°C. It's important to be patient with this step as yeast is killed off above 50°C. If you're in a hurry, you can pour the milk from one pan into another and repeat a few times, which will help to speed up the cooling process.

Pour the milk mixture into the flour mixture and add the eggs. Stir through using a large spoon and mix really well for a few minutes until it starts to resemble a rough dough.

Use a dough scraper if you have one to scrape out all the dough on to a clean work surface. Knead the dough for 10–15 minutes or until it looks smooth and springs back when you touch it. Lightly oil the bowl you mixed the dough in to begin with and place the kneaded dough back in before you cover it with a damp tea towel. Place the bowl in an airing cupboard or warm room for an hour, or until the dough has doubled in size.

When the dough has risen, preheat the oven to 220°C/gas mark 7 and have a baking tray ready (simply reuse it after each batch of baking). Place the dough on a clean work surface and, using a rolling pin (or your hands—

it's less elegant but will do the job just fine), roll the dough out to a large rectangle. Don't worry about measuring it—just give it a quick look to make sure the dough is around 1cm thick at this stage.

Mix the filling ingredients in a bowl and slather evenly across the upper horizontal half of the rectangle, then fold over the lower half so that you have a rather abnormally shaped book. Using a sharp knife, cut the dough into even slices—you should get about 25–30, depending on the thickness of the slices. Separate each slice and start to twist them by holding one end and twirling into a cruller shape. Fold this over your thumb and twist into a bun shape (sometimes they look a little disfigured but they still taste great—no need to be precious about the appearance of these buns!).

Place the first batch of twists on the baking tray, making sure they're not too close together as they will spread, and glaze with egg wash. You can decorate the twists with flaked almonds, Swedish pearl sugar or demerara sugar, or just leave them plain if you prefer. Set aside to prove for a few minutes.

When the first batch of cardamom twists is good to go—they shouldn't spring back when you poke them, but if they do just let them prove a little longer—spritz the oven with a little water and quickly place the baking tray on the upper shelf and bake at 220°C/gas mark 7 for the first 5 minutes to give them some lift-off, then reduce the temperature to 190°C/gas mark 5 for the remaining 5–10 minutes, or until they're done. They should look golden brown and sound hollow when you tap them.

Remove the twists from the oven and place them on a wire rack. If there's some cardamom butter on the baking tray, simply sweep the excess butter off and either munch on it or, if it's still hot, drizzle it on the twists for extra flavour. Repeat with the remaining batches and allow them to cool (slightly) before devouring.

*Variations. Instead of cardamom in the filling why not try a festive twist? Substitute the same amount of spice with Scandinavian pepperkake, or gingerbread spices, or indeed a classic mixed spice, or make your own. I'd always use more cinnamon, cardamom, nutmeg and err on the side of caution when it comes to ginger, cloves and black pepper, but each to their own.*

*If you'd rather have a more neutral butter filling then replace the cardamom with heady vanilla extract. You can also add a handful of ground almonds to the butter filling, along with some Scandi marzipan for a full almond experience, topping the twists with flaked almonds too.*

# Rhubarb & Orange Muffins

Makes 12 muffins

On my great-grandparents' farm there was a rhubarb patch that thrived particularly well and the long pink stalks were always popular for baking, pickling and for cooking alongside roast meats. The combination of rhubarb and orange is a classic and with good reason: they complement each other beautifully.

200g (about 3 slender sticks) rhubarb, cut into 5mm slices

2 unwaxed oranges

250g refined spelt flour (or plain flour)

75g ground almonds

185g golden caster sugar, plus extra for the rhubarb

1½ tsp baking powder

⅛ tsp bicarbonate of soda

¼ tsp fine sea salt

150g Greek yoghurt

100g butter, melted

3 eggs, lightly beaten

1 tsp vanilla extract

Red or Yellow Ribbon Grand Marnier (optional)

*Preheat* the oven to 180°C/gas mark 4 and line a 12-hole muffin tin with muffin cases. Place a shallow tray with water on a lower shelf.

Place the rhubarb in a bowl and mix with the zest and juice of 1 orange and a spoonful or two of caster sugar, or more if you like it sweeter. Stir to coat the rhubarb.

Sieve all the dry ingredients into a separate bowl and stir through so the raising agents are evenly distributed. Stir in the zest of the other orange. Make a well in the middle and add all the wet ingredients, adding a splash of Grand Marnier, if using.

Stir the mixture in a figure-of-eight pattern, making sure to scoop up the dry bits around the edges of the bowl. After about a dozen stirs, add the rhubarb, along with some of the juices from the bowl for extra flavour (or reserve them for a glaze—see Variation).

Stir the rhubarb through a few times and then use a large spoon or ice-cream scoop to dollop the mixture into the muffin cases. Bake on the middle shelf for about 20 minutes, or until the muffins have risen, look golden brown and feel firm to the touch. Remove from the oven and allow to cool on a wire rack.

*Variation: Try blood oranges when they're in season—their deep colour creates a beautiful glaze: mix the juices with some icing sugar and brush over the muffins while still warm.*

# Sour Cherry Bundt Cake

These swirly new tins make a traditional bundt cake so much fun to bake. This is my version, reminiscent of summers spent picking juicy *Kirsebær* (sour cherries) on my grandparents' farm. Sour cherries have a more intense flavour than black cherries, but they can be hard to source and black cherries will still be delicious in this recipe. Dried sour cherries can also be soaked and used in this cake if need be.

*Preheat* the oven to 170°C/gas mark 3 and thoroughly grease and lightly flour a 2.4-litre, 26 x 9.5cm bundt cake tin (I use one from Nordic Ware).

Place the dried sour cherries and maraschino cherries in a bowl and cover them with Cherry Heering. Sieve the dry ingredients from the flour to the sea salt into a separate bowl and stir through so that the baking powder is evenly distributed.

In a mixing bowl beat the butter together with the golden caster sugar until pale and fluffy, about 5–8 minutes, then add 1 of the eggs along with a spoonful of the flour mixture and beat again until the egg is fully incorporated. Repeat with the remaining 2 eggs. Then add the remaining flour mixture and gently fold in along with the vanilla extract and buttermilk. Stir until the mixture is nice and even.

Drain the cherries (keep the Cherry Heering to use for the glaze, or even for future cocktails!) and carefully fold them into the cake mixture. Once the cherries are folded in, scoop the batter into the prepared bundt tin and bake in the preheated oven for 35–40 minutes, or until a metal skewer inserted in the centre comes out clean, the top of the cake looks golden, feels springy and a little firm to the touch, and the cake is coming away slightly from the sides of the tin.

Serves 10–12

100g dried sour cherries

100g maraschino cherries
  (or fresh cherries, pitted)

Cherry Heering

225g refined spelt flour (or plain flour),
  plus extra for dusting

50g ground almonds

1½ tsp baking powder

¼ tsp fine sea salt

225g butter, at room temperature,
  plus extra for greasing

225g golden caster sugar

3 medium eggs

½ tsp vanilla extract

150ml buttermilk

150g icing sugar, for the glaze (optional)

Place the tin on a wire rack and cool for 20 minutes before turning the cake out to cool completely on the rack. If you wish to glaze the cake, simply put the icing sugar in a bowl and add a spoonful of the reserved Cherry Heering (or some cherry cordial), then stir until you have a sticky glaze to drizzle over the cake.

*Variations: Instead of cherries you can add blueberries, raspberries or chopped rhubarb to this mixture. Make this a lemon poppy seed bundt cake by adding the zest of 2 lemons to the cake mixture, and replacing the cherries with poppy seeds. Glaze with a punchy lemon drizzle by mixing 150g icing sugar with the zest of 1 lemon and the juice of ½ a small lemon, or as much as you need to make a sticky lemon glaze.*

—— *"Instead of cherries you can add blueberries, raspberries or chopped rhubarb to this mixture."*

# Dark Chocolate Muffins

Makes 12 muffins

I could write a whole book about muffins, they're so easy to prepare, versatile and delicious—a simple and quick way to enjoy fika.

150g refined spelt flour (or plain flour)

100g ground almonds

200g light brown muscovado sugar
   (or a mix of light brown and golden
   caster sugar if you prefer)

1½ tsp baking powder

¼ tsp fine sea salt

⅛ tsp bicarbonate of soda

3 medium eggs

150ml Greek yoghurt

150g butter, melted

1 tsp vanilla extract

60g good cocoa powder

1 shot espresso or strong filter coffee

150g dark chocolate chips
   (or a chocolate bar, finely chopped)

*Preheat* the oven to 180°C/gas mark 4 and line a 12-hole muffin tin with muffin cases. Place a shallow tray with water on a lower shelf.

Sieve all the dry ingredients into a mixing bowl and stir through so the raising agents are evenly distributed.

In a separate bowl, crack the eggs and lightly whisk with a fork to break them up. Add the yoghurt, butter and vanilla extract. Stir through. In another bowl, carefully mix the cocoa powder with the coffee until you have a thick paste. Scoop this into the egg mixture and stir well so you have a dark, chocolatey mixture.

Make a well in the middle of the dry ingredients and add the chocolatey egg mixture. Stir in a figure-of-eight pattern, making sure to scoop up the dry bits around the edges of the bowl. Add the dark chocolate chips and stir a few more times. Use a large spoon or ice-cream scoop to dollop the mixture into the muffin cases.

Bake on the middle shelf for about 20 minutes, or until the muffins have risen, look dark brown and feel firm to the touch. Remove from the oven and allow to cool on a wire rack.

*Variations: You can add a mix of dark, milk and white chocolate chips to the muffin mixture. Spice up the cake mixture with a little cinnamon and/or nutmeg and feel free to decorate the muffins with some flaked almonds or cocoa nibs for extra crunch.*

*Tip: We love cocoa powder in the Nordic region—Valrhona is regarded as the best.*

# Brown Butter, Sugar & Malt Shortbread

**Given my predilection for all things malt, I couldn't resist adding this biscuit recipe to the fika collection.**

*First* make the brown butter. Place a clean J-cloth or paper coffee filter in a sieve resting on top of a bowl. Melt 75g of the butter in a small saucepan until it starts to foam and separate. You need to keep an eye on it during this stage as the butter can quickly go from nutty and delicious to bitter and acrid. Keep checking the butter—it should smell nutty and little bits of caramelized milk solids will start to appear. Once they look brown (but not black) remove the saucepan from the heat and pour the butter into the sieve to remove the brown milk solids. Allow the butter to cool while you prepare the rest of the ingredients.

Cream the remaining butter with the sugar for 5 minutes, or until fluffy and paler than when you started. Add the cooled brown butter and cream again. Next add the egg along with a spoonful of flour (either one) and cream once more. Finally add the remaining ingredients and mix with a large spoon or spatula. Using your hands to bring it all together will help to give a uniform consistency to the biscuit dough.

Gently knead the dough on a clean surface then place it on a long sheet of cling film. Carefully fold the sheet of cling film over the dough and roll it into a sausage shape about 3cm in diameter. Twist the ends of the cling film so they're firmly sealed and the dough is a uniform thickness, then chill in the fridge for a few hours or in the freezer for 30–45 minutes. The colder the dough is when you come to bake the biscuits, the crisper they will be once they're baked.

Makes 30 biscuits

150g unsalted butter

75g light brown muscovado sugar

1 egg

150g refined spelt flour (or fine cake flour)

150g sprouted wholemeal spelt flour
(or wholemeal plain flour of your choice)

1 tsp baking powder

2 tbsp barley malt extract

½ tsp fine sea salt

*See photograph on page 64*

Preheat the oven to 170°C/gas mark 3 when you're ready to bake the biscuits and cover two baking trays with greaseproof paper. Remove the dough from the fridge or freezer, unwrap it, and use a very sharp knife to slice it into 30 evenly sized discs. Place them on the prepared baking trays, taking care not to crowd them in too much as they will spread during cooking.

Bake on the middle shelf for 15 minutes or until the biscuits look golden brown and feel dry to the touch. Leave them to cool on a wire rack before eating.

*Variations: Spices such as nutmeg would go well in this recipe, and if you want to add a little extra texture you could include a small handful of toasted oats or toasted chopped nuts to the dough. Dark chocolate chips would also be a fine addition.*

# Midsummer Almond Torte with a Lemon & Elderflower Glaze

**This cake is delicious served as is, or with a dollop of crème fraiche and a sprinkling of seasonal berries. It's particularly good with a glass of refreshing Scandinavian Summer Punch (page 157).**

*Preheat* the oven to 170°C/gas mark 3 and lightly grease a 23cm round cake tin, or line it with baking parchment.

Beat the egg yolks with the sugar in a mixing bowl until pale and creamy. Add the remaining ingredients and stir through with a large spoon until the mixture is even and thick. In a separate bowl, whisk the egg whites until stiff peaks form. Using a large metal spoon, add a spoonful of the egg whites to the almond mixture to loosen it before adding the remainder of the egg whites and folding them in. Be careful not to over-fold—the mixture should be quite mousse-like.

Carefully scoop the batter into the tin and bake in the middle of the oven for 30–35 minutes or until the cake has risen, looks golden brown and feels firm to the touch. Remove from the oven and cool on a wire rack for a few minutes before turning the cake out to cool completely.

Meanwhile, make the glaze: put the icing sugar in a bowl and stir in a spoonful of elderflower cordial and a little lemon zest and juice. Stir until you have a sticky glaze and gently drizzle this over the cake. Once the glaze has set slightly, sprinkle edible flowers on top to decorate.

*Variations:* *You can make this a spiced almond cake by adding a teaspoonful of mixed spice (or a combination of ground cinnamon, cardamom, nutmeg and cloves— go easy on the cloves as they have a strong medicinal pungency) to the mixture instead of the lemon zest. Spike the glaze with whisky, rum or any spirit/liqueur of your choice too for a boozy kick.*

Serves 8–10

4 medium eggs, separated
200g golden caster sugar
300g ground almonds
100g butter, melted, plus extra for greasing
zest of 1 unwaxed lemon
1 tsp vanilla extract
¼ tsp salt

*For the Glaze*
150g icing sugar
elderflower cordial
zest and juice of 1 unwaxed lemon

*To Decorate*
edible flowers (or fresh elderflowers
    if you can find them)
seasonal berries

# Cardamom Doughnuts with Orange Blossom Honey

Makes 15–20 doughnuts

We used to make these for our EatScandi supper club events, as so few people make their own doughnuts at home anymore. It felt special, and we were overjoyed to hear guests tell us it was the finest fried dough they'd ever tasted. Home-made doughnuts require a little effort, I'll admit, but if you've ever been curious about how to make them then I urge you to give these a go—they're the ultimate fika treat.

*For Stage 1*

150g strong white flour

20g fresh yeast (or 10g dried)

150ml water

*For Stage 2*

150ml whole milk

2 tsp freshly ground cardamom

15g fresh yeast

350g refined spelt flour

200g strong white flour

100g golden caster sugar

10g sea salt

6 egg yolks

*For Stage 3*

75g butter, cut into 1cm cubes

*For the Final Stage*

1 litre vegetable oil, for frying

*To Serve*

orange blossom honey

*Stage 1:* Mix the ingredients together in a large bowl and beat for 5 minutes until you have a smooth, runny paste. Cover the bowl and set it aside somewhere warm. Allow the dough to rise for 1 hour or until it's bubbling and doubled in size.

*Stage 2:* Heat the milk and cardamom until scalding and then set aside in a cold place so that the milk cools to below 50°C. It's important to be patient with this step as yeast is killed off above 50°C. If you're in a hurry, you can pour the milk from one pan into another and repeat a few times, which will help to speed up the cooling process. Crumble the fresh yeast into the flours and add to the first bowl along with the cooled cardamom-infused milk and the remainder of the ingredients in this stage. Knead well for 10–15 minutes or until the dough looks smooth and springs back when you touch it. The dough should feel quite firm and not too slippery or loose (that will come when you add the butter).

*Stage 3:* This is the most crucial stage of the whole process so please don't rush it. You need to add the cubes of butter one at a time to the dough and work the butter in completely before adding the next cube.

I know it sounds fussy but it makes a difference. If you rush this stage you'll end up with an oily dough, and what you want is a smooth, supple dough for frying. A little elbow grease should mean this process will take about 10 minutes at most, and then you can have a rest while the dough relaxes for a further 30–45 minutes. (Make sure to cover it again so that it doesn't dry out.)

*Stage 4:* Once you've had a cup of tea and allowed your arms to recover, scrape the dough on to a clean work surface and use a dough scraper or sharp knife to portion the dough into equal-sized balls. If you want to be precise about this, you can weigh the dough and then divide that amount by the number of doughnuts you wish to make, using that figure to determine the weight of each ball. Cup your hand over each dough ball and swirl it around on the work surface to create a really smooth bun shape, then place the bun on a baking tray or platter and cover with a damp tea towel while you repeat the process with the remainder of the dough balls. Put the baking tray or platter in an airing cupboard or warm room for a further 30–45 minutes—the final rising time. You'll know they're ready to be fried when they've doubled in size and they no longer spring back when you touch the dough.

*Stage 5:* Pour the oil in a deep-fryer or a large saucepan or stock pan (as a safety precaution, it shouldn't come up further than a third of the total height of the pan), and have a sugar thermometer or a digital probe ready to check the temperature of the oil. It needs to reach 160°C for the optimum doughnut-frying temperature. Keep an eye on it and have the following to hand: a long oven glove, a lid that can completely cover the pan should a fire break out and a long slotted spoon or spider spoon—plus have the ventilation on full blast otherwise your kitchen and house will smell of fried dough for a day or two afterwards!

Start to fry the doughnuts and keep an eye on the heat to make sure it doesn't rise above 170°C or dip below 150°C. (If the oil starts to seriously smoke, turn off the heat immediately and do not under any circumstances pour water on hot oil.) Fry the doughnuts for 2 minutes (if small) and up to 3–4 minutes (if large) on each side—you can flip them over using the slotted spoon. They should look even and golden-pale brown on both sides.

Once the doughnuts are cooked through, use the slotted spoon to carefully lift them out of the oil and place them on kitchen paper to drain off the excess oil. Transfer the doughnuts to a separate plate and drizzle lots of delicious orange blossom honey all over them.

*Stage 6:* Eureka! Congratulations, you've made doughnuts. It's a big moment if you've never made them before so I hope you love them as much as I do. Remember to turn off the hot oil when you finish frying.

*Variations: We often tossed the doughnuts in cardamom sugar or cinnamon sugar—just a bowl of caster sugar mixed with as much spice as you like (I like a lot—we're talking a tablespoon of the stuff but you may not be as keen on a full hit of spice) and then tossing the doughnuts in the sugar while warm. You can stuff them with summer jams such as plum, cherry, blueberry, apricot or raspberry, and of course you can glaze them with whichever favourite glaze you have but I find most sugar glazes to be so sickly sweet that I steer clear of that option. Add a shot of brandy, whisky, Grand Marnier or rum to a bowl of icing sugar, however, and then you might be on to something ...*

# Darkness & Light

Serves 8

We Johansens love a classic vanilla sponge cake. *Drømmekage*, or 'dream cake', topped with coconut salted caramel, and the popular *toscakake*, with almond salted caramel, both make it into my list of all-time favourite cakes. I wanted to try something with dark chocolate and, after a little tinkering, this was the result. Bitter chocolate offsets the light, buttery vanilla sponge— a reflection of the contrasts you find in Scandinavia's character, landscape and seasons.

*For the Sponge*

3 medium eggs

200g golden caster sugar

1 tsp vanilla extract

100g butter, melted, plus extra for greasing

100ml buttermilk

200g refined spelt flour (or fine cake flour), plus extra for dusting

1 tsp baking powder

¼ tsp fine sea salt

*For the Dark Chocolate Topping*

125g butter

125g light brown sugar

5 tbsp cocoa powder

1 shot strong coffee or espresso (optional)

1 tsp sea salt

50g cocoa nibs (optional)

*Preheat* the oven to 170°C/gas mark 3. Lightly grease and dust with flour a 23cm round cake tin or line it with baking parchment.

Whisk together the eggs, sugar and vanilla extract until thickened, pale and fluffy. This will take a good 8–10 minutes but be patient, this stage really helps give the sponge its lightness.

Add the butter, buttermilk and dry ingredients in two stages, folding in carefully with a large metal spoon in a figure-of-eight pattern so as not to knock out too much air. Gently pour the mixture into the tin and bake on the middle shelf for 25–30 minutes, or until the sponge looks golden and feels firm to the touch. It needs to be baked through before you add the topping—a skewer inserted in the centre should come out clean.

Meanwhile, melt the topping ingredients in a small saucepan over a medium heat and set aside.

Remove the cake from the oven, placing the tin on a heatproof surface. Turn the oven up to 220°C/gas mark 7. Gently pour the chocolate topping over the cake then put it back into the oven to crisp up—about 5–8 minutes, but be careful not to let it burn.

Remove the cake from the oven and leave to cool on a wire rack before turning out.

# Sticky Ginger Cake with a Clementine Glaze

Always a favourite during the yule season, I baked this on Kirstie Allsopp's *Handmade Christmas* TV programme and it was so popular I decided to include the recipe here. I'm not wild about sickly sweet marzipan or tooth-busting sugar icing on traditional British Christmas cakes, so this is my Nordic alternative —festive colours, flavours and just the right amount of sweetness to feel celebratory …

*Preheat* the oven to 170°C/gas mark 3 and lightly grease a 900g loaf tin.

Melt the butter, sugar and treacle in a medium saucepan, stir through and remove from the heat. Cool slightly then add the buttermilk and eggs.

Sieve the flours, raising agents, spices and salt into a medium bowl. Add to the liquid ingredients in the pan in stages, stirring thoroughly after each addition until evenly mixed. Pour the batter into the prepared loaf tin and bake on the middle shelf of the oven for 45 minutes, then cover with aluminium foil to prevent the top from scorching. Bake for a further 10–15 minutes or until the loaf has risen and feels firm to the touch. If in doubt, insert a metal skewer into the centre and if it comes out clean the cake is done.

Place the cake on a wire rack and allow to cool for a few minutes before turning it out and piercing the top in several places. Make a clementine glaze by mixing together the icing sugar, clementine zest and juice, and lemon juice until you have a sticky icing. It shouldn't be too runny or the glaze will just pour right off the cake. Drizzle the glaze over the ginger cake and sprinkle with pomegranate seeds and pistachios to decorate.

Serves 8–10

125g butter, plus extra for greasing

175g molasses sugar
   (or dark brown muscovado)

150ml treacle

250ml buttermilk

2 medium eggs, lightly beaten

175g refined spelt flour (or plain flour)

75g wholemeal spelt flour
   (or rye, wholewheat, oatmeal flour)

2 tsp bicarbonate of soda

1 tsp baking powder

2 tsp ground cinnamon

2 tsp freshly grated root ginger

1 tsp ground cardamom

½ nutmeg, freshly grated

½ tsp fine sea salt

*For the Glaze*

150g icing sugar

zest and juice of 1 clementine

juice of 1 lemon

*To Decorate*

seeds of 1 small pomegranate

bright green raw pistachios

# Christmas Spice Madeleines

Makes 12 madeleines

If there's a piece of baking kit I'd recommend alongside a 23cm round cake tin and a 12-hole muffin tin, it's a madeleine tray. Madeleines are so easy to make and everyone adores them—they're both delicious and pretty to look at.

125g butter, plus extra for greasing

2 tbsp maple syrup

1 shot of espresso or strong coffee

½ nutmeg, grated

½ tsp cinnamon (optional extras:
    ½ tsp ground cardamom, ⅛ tsp ground
    cloves, a few cracks of black pepper)

¼ tsp sea salt

75g icing sugar

50g refined spelt flour (or plain flour),
    plus extra for dusting

50g ground almonds

¼ tsp baking powder

3 medium egg whites

*Place* the butter in a small saucepan and melt over a low heat with the maple syrup, coffee, spice(s) and sea salt.

Sieve the icing sugar, flour, almonds and baking powder into a mixing bowl and pour in the melted butter mixture, along with the egg whites. Stir together until you have a thick batter. Cover and put in the fridge for a few hours to chill, or ideally overnight.

When you're ready to bake the madeleines, preheat the oven to 170°C/gas mark 3. Grease a 12-hole madeleine tray with butter and lightly dust with flour. Spoon even amounts of the batter into each hole, to about two-thirds full.

Bake in the oven for about 15 minutes or until the madeleines have risen, with a little dome on top, and look golden brown. Remove from the oven and allow the madeleines to cool for a minute or two before you nudge each one out of its hollow—be quick doing this as they can get stuck in the tray.

Eat while warm, or keep for later and then refresh them in the oven at 150°C/gas mark 2 for a few minutes so they crisp up again.

*Tip: If you're using a mini madeleine tray, they'll only need around 8 minutes in the oven, so keep an eye on them.*

# Malty Banana Chocolate Chip Walnut Muffins

**Children love these muffins; they're fun to assemble and have a deep flavour thanks to the malt extract. That's not to say grown-ups can't enjoy them too ...**

*Preheat* the oven to 180°C/gas mark 4 and line a 12-hole muffin tin with muffin cases. Place a shallow tray with water on a lower shelf.

Sieve all the dry ingredients into a mixing bowl and stir through so the raising agents are evenly distributed. In a separate bowl, mash the bananas with a fork. Add all the remaining liquid ingredients to the banana and stir through. Make a well in the middle of the dry ingredients and add the banana mixture.

Stir the banana muffin mixture in a figure-of-eight pattern, making sure to scoop up the dry bits around the edges of the bowl. Add the dark chocolate chips along with the walnut pieces and stir a few more times. Use a large spoon or ice-cream scoop to dollop the mixture into the muffin cases.

Bake on the middle shelf for about 20 minutes, or until the muffins have risen, look golden brown and feel firm to the touch. Remove from the oven and allow to cool on a wire rack.

*Variations: You can make plain banana muffins and omit the chocolate and walnuts. Alternatively, add other nuts such as almonds or pecans to the mixture; and a splash of maple syrup in the muffin mixture instead of the malt also gives a pleasing flavour.*

Makes 12 muffins

225g refined spelt flour (or plain flour)
50g sprouted spelt flour
   (or wholemeal flour)
100g light brown muscovado sugar
1 tsp baking powder
¼ tsp bicarbonate of soda
¼ tsp fine sea salt
¼ tsp cinnamon
3 medium bananas
75g butter, melted
75ml Greek yoghurt
2 eggs
1 tbsp barley malt
1 tsp vanilla extract
150g dark chocolate chips
   (or a chocolate bar, finely chopped)
50g walnuts, broken into pieces

# Chocolate, Almond & Marzipan Prunes

Makes 20–22

Fika doesn't always have to mean baking. I have chef Jeremy Lee to thank for the idea for these utterly addictive chocolate prunes. I tried them at his London restaurant Quo Vadis and couldn't stop thinking about how delicious they were, so I set about trying to recreate them in my kitchen at home. The secret is to use the best dark chocolate you can source, and juicy, plump Agen prunes. Enjoy with a cup of coffee, sencha tea or a snifter of whisky on a cold winter's night.

250g Agen prunes (about 20–22)

150g Scandinavian *mandelmassa*
    (almond paste) or best quality
    marzipan (at least 50% almond content)

150g dark chocolate

blanched almonds, lightly toasted
    (1 for each prune)

vanilla sea salt

*Place* the prunes on a clean chopping board and slit them open, de-stoning them if necessary. Roll the *mandelmassa* or marzipan into little balls—they need to be small enough to stuff into the prunes.

Next, place a heatproof bowl over a saucepan of very gently simmering water—make sure the water doesn't boil. Break the chocolate into small pieces and drop them into the bowl. Once the chocolate has completely melted, remove from the saucepan. To get a thin, even coating, dip the prunes into the chocolate as soon as it's melted, and place them on a wire rack if you want them to look quite neat and tidy. Pop a toasted almond on top of each chocolate prune along with a flake of vanilla sea salt and allow them to set.

*Variations: You can make a dark chocolate fruit and nut brittle by applying the same method of melting dark chocolate, then, once it has cooled a little so it thickens, drop in a handful of your favourite toasted nuts (I like a mix of almonds and walnuts) with some dried sour cherries, or just nuts alone, and gently scoop out the mixture on to a board so the chocolate brittle can set.*

# five

---

# the nordic kitchen

# Nordic by Nature

'Cooking is caring for others,' says the Danish-Icelandic artist Olafur Eliasson. Most of us intuitively grasp this; after all, to break bread with someone is a time-honoured act of kinship and solidarity. The size of this chapter reflects that core belief. Good food really doesn't have to be complicated. Although the kitchen is central to good living, the philosophy underpinning this book is that an economy of effort is the key to eating for life.

Modern Nordic cooking is based on keeping things simple, with an emphasis on naturally nourishing ingredients such as berries, wholegrains, lean meats, pickles, seasonal vegetables and sustainably sourced fish and seafood. As a wise woman once said (OK, it was my mother but she *is* wise), 'Norwegians have the healthiest fast food in the world,' and she's right: you can create the best meals using hot smoked trout, smoked salmon, gravlaks (see the Whisky-Cured Gravlaks on page 128), pickled herring, cooked North Sea prawns, lightly salted cod and much more.

Breakfast is a ritual that deserves to be treated as such. Having a few minutes in the morning to eat a healthy meal really does put you in the right frame of mind for the day ahead. I find myself completely discombobulated if I've had to rush out the door in the morning without a decent breakfast. Weekend hygge can be found in the Oatmeal Waffles on page 99 (make sure you ring-fence 25 March, or Waffle Day), and in slow-cooked dishes such as the Spiced Roast Pork Belly on page 134.

As much as I love cooking, I'd be a hypocrite if I claimed I always cooked from scratch, which is why a well-stocked pantry can make all the difference. There's something immensely satisfying about a 'fridge forage', and allowing yourself to cook a dish based solely on a few ingredients you happen to have to hand is a fun, creative exercise, but not everyone has the luxury or the mindset to do so. Don't be so hard on yourself during the week if you're too busy to cook. The salad and vegetable dishes in this chapter will hopefully allow you to rustle up something tasty in a few minutes. Most of the recipes here are meant as guides, so freestyle with ingredients and flavours as you see fit!

# Muesli
# Ne Plus Ultra

Since childhood I've been something of a muesli obsessive. Too often the commercially available ones are dusty and loaded with raisins, which I really can't stand. Good muesli has a winning balance of mixed cereal flakes, a variety of nuts, seeds and dried fruit and contrasting flavours and textures. If you're going to start your day on a healthy note, always make it delicious ...

Makes enough for
about 15–20 servings

*Place* all the ingredients in a large mixing bowl—I use about 2 tsp cinnamon—and stir together so that everything is evenly distributed. Store the muesli in a 2-litre tall glass jar with a lid.

*Variations: You can use any assortment of dried fruit that you fancy. I just love the contrast of the sour tang of dried cherries alongside the chewy sweetness of the bananas. You can also add a cupful of your favourite granola to the mixture for extra crunch (I like the coconut and chia granola from Rude Health).*

*Tip: To make your own vanilla almonds and toasted coconut, simply heat the oven to 150°C/gas mark 2 and place the raw almonds and coconut on separate baking trays. The almonds will be toasty and delicious after about 10–15 minutes (keep an eye on them as they can turn suddenly) and the coconut needs only about 5–8 minutes before it turns golden. Remove from the oven and allow to cool. When the almonds have cooled for a few minutes, stir through a teaspoonful of vanilla extract, tossing them to coat.*

550g mixed cereal flakes
   (I use oats, rye, barley and spelt)
180g toasted vanilla almonds (see Tip)
180g chewy dried bananas (Bogoya
   sun-dried ones are best)
180g dried sour cherries
180g omega seed mix
   (I use linseed, pumpkin,
   sesame and sunflower)
100g toasted coconut flakes (see Tip)
ground cinnamon, to taste

See photograph on page 92

# Coconut Oatmeal Porridge

Serves 2

A highlight of my food career was coming joint first in the London Porridge Championships. Grains are ingrained (sorry, couldn't resist!) in a typical Nordic breakfast routine and we love porridge, or cooked oatmeal. There are many ways to jazz up a bowl of porridge, but having a predilection for all things coconut this was the version I entered. It was voted joint winner alongside arctic explorer Christina Franco's savoury bacon and egg porridge.

100g pinhead oatmeal

150ml coconut water

150ml coconut milk

75ml coconut cream

¼ tsp vanilla salt

(I use Halen Môn vanilla salt)

Fruits of the Forest Compote (page 97)

or simply use fresh berries if you prefer

*Start* by soaking the oatmeal in the coconut water the night before you want to make the porridge. This helps the grains soften and swell, making a much creamier porridge the next day.

In the morning, place the coconut milk and coconut cream in a small saucepan. Bring to the boil and add the soaked oatmeal. Turn the heat down to a gentle simmer and keep stirring for 5–10 minutes until the porridge thickens. If it gets too thick, just add a little more coconut water (plain will also do) or coconut milk or cream. Add the vanilla salt, stir through and taste. If you like a slightly more savoury porridge, just add a pinch or two more of salt and keep stirring. You need to let the salt melt completely, so don't be tempted to rush this stage otherwise you'll be crunching on salt crystals.

Once the porridge is cooked to the consistency you like, remove the pan from the hob and let the porridge settle for a minute. Pour it into two bowls and top with a mixed berry compote or fresh berries, along with any other toppings you fancy—nuts, maple syrup, spices, a pat of good butter all work really well.

*Variation: This is a dairy-free recipe but you can of course make it with whole milk and double cream.*

# Nordic Berry, Omega & Kefir Smoothie

At least once a week I'll start the day with a berry smoothie, and although there are infinite variations the key is to have a balance of sweet and sour, make it very cold and add some nut butters to cut through the sharpness of the berries. This is a brilliant smoothie with vital fats when you just need to down something nourishing in a hurry, or have to take your breakfast on the road.

*Place* all the ingredients in a blender and pulse for a few seconds to break up the berries and banana. Then blend until you have a smooth, purple smoothie. Taste it before you serve and add more lemon juice or berries if it's too bland, or some ice if it's a bit sweet.

*Variation: Kefir is a probiotic milk drink originally from the Caucasus mountains; you could use plain drinking yoghurt instead.*

Serves 2

1 small punnet (about 150g) blueberries

1 small punnet (about 150g) raspberries

250ml kefir

2 small bananas

2 tbsp omega seed mix (I use linseed, pumpkin, sesame and sunflower)

1 tbsp nut butter of your choice (almond, cashew, peanut all work well)

juice of 1 lemon (and a little zest if you like lemon)

1 tsp  honey or maple syrup (or more if the bananas aren't quite ripe)

1 tsp freshly grated ginger

pinch of ground cinnamon

ice cubes, to serve (optional—only use if the berries and bananas aren't frozen)

# Fruits of the
# Forest Compote

Makes about 500g

Fresh berries are such a highlight during the short summer season. But this is a way to cheat a taste of summer during the dark winter months. It's an easy compote to rustle up, especially if you always have a bag of frozen berries to hand, and makes a wonderful accompaniment to the porridge, pancakes and waffles in this chapter.

100g fruit sugar (or 150g caster sugar)

75ml water

5 cardamom pods

1 star anise

1 cinnamon stick

1 strip of peel and juice of 1 unwaxed orange

1 strip of peel and juice of 1 unwaxed lemon

450g bag of mixed frozen berries

*See photograph on page 98*

*Start* by making a spiced sugar syrup: bring the sugar and water to a simmer in a small saucepan. Allow the sugar to dissolve completely and then remove the pan from the heat. Add the spices and zests of orange and lemon and allow to infuse for 1 hour, or leave overnight if you'd prefer to stagger the prep for this.

Next, in a medium saucepan sieve the sugar syrup to remove the spices and citrus peel. Add the juice of the orange and lemon and bring to a simmer over a low-medium heat, adding the fruit and cooking over a medium heat until the berries burst and the compote thickens.

Finally, remove the pan from the heat and allow the compote to cool completely before refrigerating, or use it immediately if you don't mind it warm.

*Variation: You can apply the same formula to fresh plums. The really tough, unripe ones benefit hugely from being converted into a compote like this.*

# Oatmeal
# Waffles

Serves 4–6

Who doesn't love a waffle? In the Nordic countries, they're traditionally made in heart-shaped irons that not only look pretty but are also ideal for sharing. An update on the classic sour cream and vanilla waffles you find in Norway, these have a nutty flavour thanks to the light toasting of oats before you blend them into a finer oatmeal. They make an excellent mid-afternoon fika, too.

150g porridge oats

350g refined spelt flour
   (or use a sprouted version if you
   want a nuttier, wholegrain flavour)

1 tsp baking powder

100g caster sugar

½ tsp sea salt

150g butter, melted, plus extra for greasing

100ml water

250g crème fraiche or sour cream

200ml oat milk (or whole milk)

4 medium eggs

2 tsp vanilla extract

*Preheat* the oven to 170°C/gas mark 3. Spread the oats on a baking tray or in an ovenproof dish and put in the oven for 10 minutes, or until the oats start to smell nutty and turn a slightly darker colour. Remove and allow to cool for a few minutes before placing half in a blender and blitzing to make a fine oat flour.

Next, sift the dry ingredients including the oat flour and toasted oats into a large mixing bowl. Make a well in the middle and add the liquid ingredients. Using a large whisk, stir well until you have a thick batter—it should take a couple of seconds to drop from the whisk.

Set the batter aside for at least 30 minutes to allow the starch cells in the flour to swell—this will help thicken the batter and produce better waffles. Spread a little butter over both the top and bottom of your waffle iron and heat, following the manufacturer's instructions. Once it's hot, place a ladleful of batter in the iron before closing. The waffles will look golden brown and crisp when they're ready. Flick them out of the iron with a palette knife and serve with toppings of your choice, for example Fruits of the Forest Compote (page 97).

*Tip: If you're not cooking the waffles at a table with your family and friends, preheat the oven to low so that you can keep them warm until you're ready to serve everyone.*

# Pancakes

**These little light-as-a-cloud pancakes are ideal for weekend brunches, especially when you're planning a long swim, a day of skiing up in the mountains or a walk outdoors and need sustenance to keep you going throughout the day. The quark makes them a good source of protein.**

Serves 2

*Place* the quark in a medium bowl, then add the milk and melted butter. Stir well before adding the egg yolks. Stir the mixture really well again to thoroughly combine.

Next add the vanilla, followed by the flour and honey, and finally the salt. Stir again until the mixture is even and looks quite thick.

In a separate bowl beat the egg whites until stiff peaks form. Add a spoonful to the quark mixture to loosen it. Then fold in the remainder of the egg white, carefully swirling your spoon or spatula in figure-of-eight movements so that you don't knock out all the air in the mixture. Stop once the egg white is folded in.

Drizzle a spoonful of oil into a pancake pan or skillet and place over a medium heat. Depending on how large your pan is, drop in 2–3 dollops of mixture once the oil is hot, with enough space so they don't merge into one another. Cook for 1–2 minutes on each side and then stack the pancakes on a plate in a warm oven while you finish the rest. (The first pancakes may be a little greasy, but don't fret, they improve with each batch.)

Serve warm with fresh berries, some Greek yoghurt, a dusting of cinnamon and a drizzle of honey or syrup of your choice.

*Variation:* You can add a mashed banana to the mixture for extra sweetness.

200g quark (you can also use
    fromage frais or ricotta)
100ml whole milk
50g butter, melted
2 medium eggs, separated
1 tsp vanilla extract
85g sprouted spelt flour
    (or flour of your choice)
2 tbsp clear honey or maple syrup,
    plus extra to drizzle
½ tsp sea salt
1 tbsp vegetable oil, for frying

*To Serve*
handful of mixed berries such as
    strawberries, raspberries, blueberries,
    blackberries, cherries
Greek yoghurt
ground cinnamon

# Smoked Salmon on Rye with Avocado, Pickled Shallot & Beets

**Salty, smoky, sour, earthy, nutty, sweet—what more can you ask from an open sandwich? This is delicious and nutritious Nordic fare at its best.**

Serves 2

*Halve* the avocado, discard the stone and cut into small pieces. Place the avocado in a bowl and add the shallot. Mix in the capers along with the lemon zest and juice and season to taste with a little salt and pepper.

Fold 2 slices of the smoked salmon on each rye bread and then scatter the avocado and shallot mixture on top. Garnish with some chopped beetroot and serve.

*Variations: Borage, parsley, chive, shiso leaf and dill all work well with this dish.*

1 avocado

1 pickled shallot (page 138), finely chopped

1 tbsp capers, rinsed and finely chopped

zest and juice of 1 unwaxed lemon

4 slices of smoked salmon

2 slices of rye bread

salt and freshly ground black pepper

pickled beetroot, finely chopped, to garnish

# Chicken Liver Pâté on Rye with Pink Grapefruit Marmalade

Serves 2

butter

2 slices of rye bread

1 pack of chicken liver pâté
    (or any pâté you prefer)

2 tsp pink grapefruit marmalade

pickled beetroot, finely chopped

1 sprig of rosemary, to garnish

Foodies often claim to love offal ... well, this one isn't so keen. But chicken liver pâté is a childhood favourite of mine and I get cravings for it every once in a while. The sharp, earthy flavours offset the salty liver flavour of the pâté.

*Generously* butter the rye bread (if it's a couple of days old, toast or refresh it in a 150°C/gas mark 2 oven for a few minutes to bring it back to life).

Spread a serious amount of chicken liver pâté on each slice of rye, then a small amount of pink grapefruit marmalade followed by a scattering of pickled beet. Strip the rosemary leaves off the sprig and finely chop before sprinkling these over the top.

# North Sea Prawns & Sourdough Crispbread Bites

**Serves 2**
**(or more as a light canapé)**

butter

1 small box of Peter's Yard mini
    sourdough crispbread

250g Norwegian cooked prawns
    with their shells on, peeled

good-quality mayonnaise

½ cucumber, shaved into thin
    ribbons or julienned

1 small jar of lumpfish roe

1 small bunch of fresh dill

1 unwaxed lemon

Sweet North Sea prawns, delicate cucumber ribbons, zingy lemon, aromatic dill and salty lumpfish roe make this snack more than the sum of its parts. Snack heaven at any time of the day, any time of the year.

*Butter* each mini crispbread and then arrange a few prawns on top. Garnish with small amounts (or a lot, who am I to judge?) of mayonnaise, cucumber, lumpfish roe, dill and a little spritz of lemon juice along with a bit of the zest.

Eat immediately. If you're not planning on going for a long swim or skiing down a mountain afterwards then a glass of cool, crisp Riesling is a fine match for this snack.

∞

Previous page—Clockwise from top left: *Chicken Liver Pâté on Rye with Pink Grapefruit Marmalade* (page 103); *Smoked Salmon on Rye with Avocado, Pickled Shallot & Beets* (page 102); *Smoked Venison on Sourdough with Pear, Fig & Toasted Nuts* (page 107); *Goat's Curd with Green Apple, Pomegranate & Acacia Honey* (page 108); *North Sea Prawns & Sourdough Crispbread Bites* (above)

# Smoked Venison on Sourdough with Pear, Fig & Toasted Nuts

Serves 2

2 decent slices of sourdough bread

butter (or olive oil)

4 slices of smoked venison

1 ripe pear, cored and sliced

1 ripe fresh fig or a couple of
   dried figs, sliced

sticky balsamic vinegar glaze

1 sprig of thyme

small handful of toasted pistachios
   and walnuts

This is a combination of robust flavours that lends itself especially to the cooler months. The mellow sweetness of pear and fig works so well with the smoky darkness of the venison.

*Toast* the sourdough bread until golden and crisp. Generously butter the toast and then layer the smoked venison on top, garnishing with slices of pear and fig before drizzling with a little balsamic glaze. Sprinkle thyme leaves on top along with the pistachios and walnuts before eating.

*Variations: You can adapt this easily into a salad by adding some roast sweet potatoes, purple sprouting broccoli, avocado, watercress and pickled shallots or fennel. And give other nuts—such as toasted almonds, hazelnuts and pecans—a try too.*

# Goat's Curd with Green Apple, Pomegranate & Acacia Honey

Being omnivorous I eat pretty much everything, but I enjoy the creative challenge of coming up with vegetarian dishes and find you have to be more inventive with flavours when you cut out meat or fish. When my colleague, now close friend, Hannah Forshaw and I ran the EatScandi supper club we would make this vegetarian canapé for our guests and it was always a hit.

Serves 2–4
(depending on how hungry you are)

*Line* up all the crispbread minis on a clean bread board and slather the goat's curd evenly on each one. I find if you make a little hollow in the curd the garnishes sit better.

Fill each hollow with chopped apple and pomegranate seeds then drizzle with a little honey. Scatter over some vanilla sea salt and, finally, place a small edible flower on top.

*Variations: You can adapt this recipe to make a larger sandwich, or even a salad. Use herbs such as basil, mint, thyme, oregano, chive or borage instead of the edible flowers. And try other fruit such as pear, fig, dried apricot, dried sour cherries or fresh raspberries in the summer months. Slivers of blood orange make a beautiful garnish in midwinter.*

1 box of Peter's Yard mini crispbread
1 tub of goat's curd
1 green apple, finely chopped or julienned
seeds of ½ pomegranate
acacia honey
vanilla sea salt
edible flowers such as pansies
    and nasturtiums (or some fresh
    herbs of your choice)

# Allspice &
# Whisky Chicken
# Skewers

Serves 2–4
(depending on how hungry you are)

'You know, I don't think that they
have enough meats on sticks.'
*There's Something About Mary*

I adore chicken skewers, a legacy from time
spent at Izakayas in Tokyo eating endless variations on yakitori. These al spiced chicken skewers are given a little kick with the addition of
Scandi Abba anchovies, whisky and cayenne
pepper and make a wonderful snack with a glass
of ice-cold beer, or indeed a whisky soda.

4 chicken thighs with skin on, bone
    removed, cut into finger-length strips
8 allspice berries, finely crushed in a pestle
    and mortar (or 1 teaspoon ground allspice)
2 Abba anchovy fillets, finely chopped
2 tbsp clear honey
50ml mild whisky
pinch of cayenne pepper
    (or more if you like things hot)
vegetable oil
salt and freshly ground black pepper

*To Serve*
fresh salad leaves of your choice
pickled rhubarb (page 138)

*I* find the easiest way to marinate meat is to use a large
transparent plastic bag instead of a bowl. With a bag you
can really massage the marinade into the meat so that
you get the most out of the marinating process. Place the
chicken strips, allspice, anchovies, honey, whisky and
cayenne pepper in the plastic bag and drizzle in enough
oil to cover everything. Squeezing out any excess air, tie
a knot in the bag, massage the meat so all the ingredients
marinate the chicken, then refrigerate for a few hours, or
overnight. If using wooden skewers, make sure to soak
them in water while you're refrigerating the chicken.

Preheat the grill to medium-high or have a barbecue
ready for the chicken skewers. Remove the chicken from
the bag of marinade, and season with salt and freshly
ground black pepper.

Grill for 5–10 minutes or so, turning the skewers
regularly so you get an even browning of the chicken.

Serve with some fresh salad leaves and a few rhubarb
pickles alongside to cut through the delicious chicken.

*Tip: The marinade also works well with pork or lamb.*

# Nordic Winter Salad

Kale is about as zeitgeisty as a winter green can be, but I'm actually not a huge fan and this is the only way I'll eat it as I find raw kale hard to chew. The secret is to really massage kale leaves so they start to soften and wilt. Roast squash or sweet potato make pretty much any salad better and pomegranate adds a little razzmatazz to this otherwise super-simple dish.

Serves 4 as a side dish,
2 as a main

*Preheat* the oven to 200°C/gas mark 6. Chop the squash or sweet potatoes into bite-sized chunks, put them on a baking tray, drizzle with olive oil, season with salt and pepper and roast in the oven for about 30 minutes or until tender. Once cooked, remove from the oven and set aside.

Place the pomegranate seeds in a bowl. Massage the kale with the lemon zest and juice and some olive oil so that the leaves soften, then add to the bowl with the pomegranate seeds. Toss together, cover and set aside until ready to serve.

Mix the salad with the roasted butternut squash and serve with some roast fish, chicken or meat of your choice. This salad also works a treat with diced feta, avocado and mixed seeds if you would rather keep it vegetarian.

1 butternut squash or 2 sweet potatoes
olive oil
seeds of 1 pomegranate
1 bunch of variegated or plain kale,
    washed and finely chopped
zest and juice of 1 large unwaxed lemon
salt and freshly ground black pepper

# The Ultimate Grilled Cheese

Serves 2

150g Jarlsberg Reserve (or Comté, Gruyère, Maasdam), coarsely grated

30g jamón ibérico, finely sliced (optional)

30g toasted hazelnuts, coarsely crushed

1 small bunch of chives

1 small bunch of parsley

a few sage leaves (optional)

1 banana shallot, finely chopped

½ tsp mustard powder (or you can use grainy mustard instead)

Worcestershire sauce and/or Tabasco sauce, to taste (I find a few drops usually does it but you may prefer it spicier)

pinch of smoked paprika and/or cayenne pepper, to taste

4 slices of sourdough bread

25g clarified butter

**Who doesn't love a grilled cheese sandwich?**

*Place* all the cheese filling ingredients up to the sourdough bread in a bowl and stir together so you have an even mixture. You can either grill or fry the sandwiches. Either way you'll need the clarified butter. If you decide to grill them simply butter the outside of each slice of sourdough and divide the filling mixture equally between the two base layers. Top with the other two slices of bread and then place them under a medium-hot grill. Cook for 2–3 minutes on each side, keeping an eye on the bread to make sure it doesn't burn. If you decide to fry the sandwiches, simply place the clarified butter in a medium-hot frying pan and cook for the same amount of time on each side. The bread should be golden brown and crisp on the outside, while the filling should be oozing and spilling out a little indecently.

Serve while hot, being careful not to bite in too soon after cooking as you'll have piping hot cheese to contend with! Serve with pickles, a salad or nourishing vegetable soup for a more substantial meal.

# Roast Cauliflower, Spinach & Blue Cheese Salad with Cherries & Walnuts

During the autumn and winter months I frequently make some variation on this salad—the nuttiness of roast cauliflower adds a pleasing warmth. You can mix it up and use roast sweet potato instead, or a mix of cooked broccoli and Brussels sprouts for a super-green salad.

*Preheat* the oven to 200°C/gas mark 6. Pop the cauliflower florets into a roasting tin, drizzle with the oil and sprinkle with salt and pepper. Roast in the oven for 30 minutes or until the cauliflower looks golden brown and has some crispy bits (these are great for munching on while you assemble the salad).

Divide the spinach between two plates and arrange the cauliflower (it can still be warm) on top of the leaves. Next, scatter over the cheese, sour cherries and walnuts and, if you like, a drizzle of oil and vinegar of your choice, or just leave the salad plain if you prefer.

Serve with slices of buttered sourdough or rye.

Serves 2

1 head of cauliflower, broken into florets

2 tbsp olive oil, plus extra to serve (optional)

1 small pack of baby spinach

100g blue cheese, crumbled

handful of dried sour cherries

handful of walnuts

sea salt and freshly ground black pepper

cherry vinegar or vinegar of your choice,
    to serve (optional)

# Nordic
# Coleslaw

This is a great dish to serve for a crowd, if you're having friends or family round for a meal or as part of a buffet-style spread. It goes with most things but is especially good with meat dishes and seafood.

*Start* by making the dressing. Mix all the ingredients together in a bowl, adjusting the seasoning to your taste. Remember, the vegetables are raw and quite bland so you want a dressing with a good punchy flavour.

Next, place the vegetables in a large bowl and add the dressing. Use two large spoons or forks (or indeed your hands—sometimes that's the easiest) and stir the dressing through the sliced vegetables so they're fully coated.

Cover the coleslaw with cling film and refrigerate for a few hours to allow the flavours to develop.

Serves a large group at a party

*For the Slaw*
1 white cabbage, finely sliced
1 celeriac, finely sliced
1 large fennel or 2 smaller ones, finely sliced
4 large carrots, finely sliced

*For the Dressing*
300g crème fraiche (you can also use sour
    cream or Greek yoghurt if you prefer)
150ml olive oil (or more if you like)
100ml salad cream (optional—but I like it)
zest and juice of 3 unwaxed lemons
4 spring onions, finely sliced (or two
    banana shallots, finely chopped)
3–4 tbsp hot horseradish sauce
3–4 tbsp white wine or cider vinegar
1 tbsp grainy mustard
2 x 15g packs of fresh dill, finely chopped
1 bunch of parsley, finely chopped
1 tbsp caraway seeds
1 tsp coriander seeds
½ tsp white pepper
sea salt

*See photograph on page 91*

# Celeriac, Potato & Mushroom Gratin

Serves 4

Winter cries out for some form of potato gratin and this is a variation on a classic. I love a creamy potato dish yet find this dairy-free version just as satisfying, but if you feel it needs a little richness replace 200ml of the stock with crème fraiche. A sprinkle of cheese or cooked bacon over the top towards the end of the cooking time also adds an extra dose of indulgence.

butter, for greasing

1 medium white onion, finely chopped

1 tbsp vegetable oil

2 medium waxy potatoes

1 small celeriac, peeled and quartered

handful of thinly sliced brown mushrooms,
    sautéed until golden brown

2 sprigs of thyme

salt and freshly ground black pepper

500ml chicken stock

*See photograph on page 137*

*Preheat* the oven to 190°C/gas mark 5 and butter a 20 x 30cm ovenproof dish.

In a small saucepan sweat the onion in the oil for about 5–8 minutes, or until soft and translucent.

Chop the potatoes and celeriac into 5mm slices (a mandoline is ideal for this, but mind your fingers when using it) and lay a third of the slices in the bottom of the ovenproof dish, then spread some of the onion and cooked mushrooms on top, along with some thyme leaves and a little salt and pepper. Repeat the process until you have filled the dish.

Pour in the hot stock (depending on how large the potatoes and celeriac are, you may not need all the stock or you may need to top up with a bit of water) until it covers all the vegetables and scatter a few more thyme leaves on the surface before placing in the hot oven and cooking for 45–60 minutes, or until the potato and celeriac are cooked through and look golden brown on top.

# Roasted Baby Squash Stuffed with Pearled Spelt & Cheese

Small squash make the ideal vessel for a warming dish like this. It's the sort of thing you can rustle up with a few ingredients from the fridge and store cupboard, so don't feel you have to follow this recipe to a T. If you're not partial to spelt grains, you can use your favourite beans or lentils instead.

Serves 1

*Preheat* the oven to 180°C/gas mark 4.

In a small sauté pan cook the shallot in the oil over a low heat until soft and translucent, about 3–5 minutes. Add the garlic and cook for a further 30–60 seconds—you don't want to burn the garlic, just soften it. Then add the pearled spelt, crème fraiche and cheese. Allow the cheese to melt and create a sauce; if it looks too thick, dilute it with either a little warm water or stock, or more crème fraiche if you like it extra-creamy. Add the sage and stir. Finally, taste and check the seasoning.

To assemble the dish, carefully slice off the top of the squash, about 2–3cm from the top, and keep the 'lid' to cover it when roasting. Scoop out the seeds (keep them for roasting later—just wash clean, allow to dry and then toss in a spiced salt or sweet mixture of your choice). Spoon the cheese mixture into the hollowed-out squash and press down to completely fill the cavity. Sprinkle a little extra cheese on top along with some salt and pepper and replace the lid. Place the squash in a roasting tin and cook for 60 minutes, or until the squash is tender. If you wish, you can add another sprinkling of grated cheese underneath the lid and place under a hot grill for a few minutes for an extra dose of cheese. Eat while warm.

1 banana shallot, finely chopped
1 tsp vegetable oil
1 small garlic clove, finely chopped
2–3 tbsp cooked pearled spelt
2–3 tbsp crème fraiche (or more if you like a creamy mixture)
small handful of grated cheese such as Cheddar, Parmesan, Jarlsberg, Gruyère—or a mix of all these!—plus extra to sprinkle on top
a few fresh sage leaves, chopped
1 baby squash (about the diameter of your hand stretched out)
salt and freshly ground black pepper

# Crispy Cod Cheeks with Nordic Dill Salsa

Cod is king along the Norwegian coastline and we pride ourselves on having the most sustainable cod fisheries in the world. Cod cheeks have a meaty succulence which makes them perfect for coating in panko breadcrumbs, frying and serving with a punchy sweet and sour dipping salsa. I love serving this at parties —hot, crispy cod cheeks are always a hit and they're terrific washed down with a glass of aquavit, or something dry and sparkling.

*Start* with the dill salsa. Place all the ingredients in a blender or Magimix and pulse several times to break down the herbs. Once the leaves are starting to compress, blitz everything together for about 1–2 minutes, or until the sauce is evenly blended. If it's quite chunky, simply let it down with a little water and/or lemon juice.

Cover the salsa with cling film and set aside while you prepare the cod cheeks. If there are any that are larger than bite-size then slice them in half. Have an assembly line ready with one bowl of seasoned flour, another with the eggs and a third with the breadcrumbs. Dip each cheek first in the flour, dusting off any excess, and then in the egg, and finally in the breadcrumbs. Set aside on a platter while you prepare them all.

Heat the deep-fryer to 160°C, or heat oil in a large saucepan to the same temperature. Fry about 6–7 cod cheek pieces at a time for about 1–2 minutes, or until they turn golden caramel. Remove from the oil with a large slotted spoon and drain on kitchen paper, then sprinkle with sea salt and pop in a warm oven while you cook the rest. Serve warm with the dill salsa.

Serves a crowd

For the Cod Cheeks

1kg cod cheeks

150g plain flour, generously seasoned

3 large eggs, lightly beaten

350g bag of panko breadcrumbs
    (I recommend JFC breadcrumbs)

salt and freshly ground black pepper


For the Nordic Dill Salsa

1 large bunch of dill

1 small bunch of parsley

½ tin Abba anchovies

50g homemade or Scandinavian
    pickled cucumbers (page 138)

1 tsp capers, rinsed

zest and juice of 1 large unwaxed lemon

3–4 tbsp olive oil

1 tsp horseradish sauce (or about 1cm
    freshly grated horseradish)


2 litres vegetable oil, for deep-frying

sea salt, to garnish

# Lightly Cured Halibut with Lemon, Riesling & Elderflowers

It's not just the Peruvians who love a fast fish cure; we have a penchant for light ceviche-style cures that sing of summer and relaxed, no-cook evenings outdoors. My parents spent a decade living in Germany and their love of German Riesling wine has definitely been passed down to me. Serve this with a chilled glass of German or Austrian Riesling as a starter.

*Slice* the halibut into 5mm thick pieces, as if you were slicing salmon for gravlaks, and arrange in a large bowl. In a separate bowl, mix the Riesling vinegar, fructose and lemon zest, and season to taste. It should taste quite sweet and sharp; if there's not enough kick to the Riesling vinegar then add the juice of your zested lemon. Pour this over the halibut slices and, using your hands, gently mix the marinade into the fish, being careful not to break up the flesh. Chill in the fridge for 20 minutes and serve either arranged on a long platter or on individual plates. Sprinkle dried elderflowers on top of the cured halibut and serve with pickles.

Serves 6 as a light starter,
more as a canapé

600g halibut, skinned and boned
150–200ml Riesling vinegar
3 tbsp fructose (fruit sugar)
zest of 1 unwaxed lemon, plus the juice
(optional)
salt and freshly ground black pepper
dried elderflowers, to garnish

To Serve
pickled cucumbers or a mix of seasonal
fresh pickles such as celery, radish
and courgettes (page 138)

# Roast Haddock with Bacon & Rye Crisp

This is a dish that came about when I worked with the Norwegian Seafood Council on recipe development. The bacon brings a savoury depth to the crisp topping and the rye bread adds crunch along with a sweet earthiness. In the colder months, steamed winter greens work really well as an accompaniment, but it's also delicious in the brighter months with a cool salad, some pickles and a glass of Pinot Noir or Beaujolais.

Serves 6

*Toast* the rye bread slices on a wire rack in a low oven for 20 minutes (thin slices) or up to 40 minutes (chunky). If the bread is already stale, simply blitz in a blender or Magimix and set aside.

Heat the oil in a frying pan and fry the bacon in two batches until crisp and the fat has rendered. Remove from the pan and drain on kitchen paper. Keep the bacon fat left in the pan.

Allow the bacon to cool completely, then break into pieces and blitz in a blender or Magimix to a fine consistency. Remove from the blender and blitz the rye bread (if you haven't already done so) to a similar consistency. Mix the bacon and rye bread in a bowl and drizzle over some of the bacon fat from the frying pan to bring the mixture together.

Crank up the oven to 200°C/gas mark 6 and place the haddock in a roasting dish, spacing the fillets evenly apart. Rub them with a little oil and season with a little salt and lots of pepper, then sprinkle the bacon rye mixture on top. Roast in the oven for 10–15 minutes, depending on the thickness of the haddock—if you cut into it, the flesh should look opaque. Serve immediately with some greens or sea vegetables, or a seasonal salad.

250g rye bread (I use Biona organic rye bread; a Danish or German-style dark rye is best for this recipe)
1 tbsp vegetable oil, plus extra for greasing
200g smoked streaky bacon
6 x 150–170g haddock fillets
salt and freshly ground black pepper
seasonal greens or sea vegetables, or salad of your choice, to serve

# Skrei Cod on Sourdough

Serves 2

1 ripe avocado

a few ripe plum or 6 cherry tomatoes,
   finely chopped

zest and juice of 1 small unwaxed lemon

Tabasco Habanero sauce

1 tsp vegetable oil

2 individual skrei fillets (skin on)

2 slices of good sourdough

salt and freshly ground black pepper

*To Serve*

parsley, thyme, chervil and/or chives

1 unwaxed lemon (optional)

**Skrei cod is a Norwegian variety fished around the Lofoten Islands which has a short season, from January to March every year. This version of avocado on toast, which we've been eating in this family for ages and has become a bit of a social media cliché, never gets old. Some dishes are timeless.**

*Slice* the avocado in half, remove the stone and scoop out the flesh into a bowl. Smash using a fork, then add the tomatoes, lemon zest and juice, a few dashes of Tabasco Habanero and salt and pepper to taste.

Next, place a medium sauté pan on the hob and drizzle in the oil. Heat until the oil sizzles. Pat the fish skin dry with kitchen paper, sprinkle with salt and pepper and place them skin side down in the hot oil. Depending on how thick the fillets are, you'll need to sauté them for about 5–8 minutes or longer until the flesh is nearly completely opaque. Season the top of the fish and, using a spatula or fish slice, carefully turn the fish over and finish cooking for a minute or so. Toast the sourdough and place on two plates. Top with equal amounts of smashed avocado, then gently place the skrei fillets on top and sprinkle over some fresh herbs. If you like extra heat, simply drizzle more Tabasco Habanero on top. An extra spritz of lemon zest and lemon juice wouldn't go amiss either, but that's up to you.

# Salmon Burgers

Serves 6

The Nordic region is famous for salmon, and I have to confess that as a kid I really, really hated the taste of cooked salmon. I was fine with smoked salmon, salmon sashimi and pretty much any other cooked fish variety but my poor mother had to suffer years of me turning my nose up at her delicious baked salmon. If only she had made salmon burgers like these I might have been converted sooner ...

800g salmon, cut into bite-sized chunks

1 tbsp mustard

1 tbsp horseradish sauce

2 anchovies

zest of 1 unwaxed lemon

handful of breadcrumbs

2 tbsp chopped spring onion

1 tsp capers

1 tsp wasabi powder

1 tsp chilli flakes or

   1 small green chilli, sliced

salt and freshly ground black pepper

oil, for greasing

*To Serve*

500ml Greek yoghurt

1 bunch of dill, finely chopped

1 bunch of chives, finely chopped

½ cucumber, deseeded and shredded

pita breads

pickled radish, fennel and cucumber

   (page 138)

*In* a blender process a quarter of the salmon along with the mustard, horseradish, anchovies and lemon zest until you have a very smooth paste. This forms the glue for the remainder of the burger mixture. Add the rest of the salmon, along with the breadcrumbs, spring onion, capers, wasabi powder and chilli. Season to taste (you can take a spoonful and pan-fry it to check the seasoning before cooking). Pulse everything together until the mixture is even, but be careful not to overmix the salmon—the fish should still be about 5mm in size.

Shape into burger patties and chill for at least 30 minutes or up to 3–4 hours before grilling.

If barbecuing, a Flip N Easy basket will help you control the cooking time, and the burgers can all be turned at the same time. Lightly oil the metal grids to prevent the burgers from sticking during cooking (this goes for an oven grill too).

Get the embers going and wait until they turn ash grey before barbecuing—avoiding an open flame is key to preventing any salmon oil spitting and creating excessive smoke. Grill until golden brown on each side and serve while hot. Simply mix the Greek yoghurt with the herbs and cucumber and serve with the pita breads and pickles.

*Tip: A side salad is optional but makes a good palate cleanser to these more-ish burgers.*

# Whisky-Cured Gravlaks

**The traditional gravlaks cure is given a boozy, festive kick with the addition of whisky. It should be slightly more sweet than salty, but you can always use equal quantities of sugar and salt if you prefer. Always source the freshest possible salmon for this dish. If in doubt, freeze the fillet for 24 hours to kill any bacteria, then defrost it.**

Serves 8 as a starter

*Dry* the salmon, check for pin bones and then lay the fillet halves side by side, skin down, on a double layer of cling film. Crush the peppercorns and coriander in a pestle and mortar and then mix in a small bowl with the sugar and salt. Spread the whisky, then the dill over the skinless side of the salmon, then spread the spiced sugar and salt mix in a layer on top. Sandwich both fillets together so that the dill and spice mixture is in the middle and the skin is outermost. Cover any exposed surface of salmon with any dill and spice mixture that tumbles out. Wrap very tightly in the two layers of cling film and place in a small roasting tin to catch the brine that escapes the fish as it cures. Refrigerate for a minimum of 24 hours and up to 48 hours.

Remove the gravlaks from the fridge, unwrap, wipe the fillet halves clean of the herby spiced salt with kitchen paper, pat dry and put on a board, skin down. Put a layer of chopped dill on the skinless side of each fillet and press down as much as you can without squashing the fish. Slice on the diagonal from the tail towards the middle and serve with sourdough crispbreads. And butter, always butter.

*Tip: If you're feeling adventurous, try adding beetroot, other alcohols (such as aquavit, cognac, gin or vodka) or juniper berries to the cure.*

1.5kg salmon fillet, cut in half
1 tbsp white peppercorns
2 tbsp coriander seeds
100g granulated sugar
75g sea salt
1 shot of whisky
3 x 15g packs of dill, chopped

*To Serve*
15g pack of dill, chopped
200g pack of Peter's Yard
    sourdough crispbread
butter

*See photograph on page 90*

# Spiced Salt
# Cod Fritters

Makes 25–30 bite-sized fritters

125g butter

200g refined spelt flour (or plain flour)

250ml whole milk

5 medium eggs

200g salt cod, soaked for 24 hours,
    patted dry and shredded

1 small tin Abba anchovies, finely sliced

1 tbsp finely chopped dill

1 tsp ground allspice

½ tsp white pepper

2 litres vegetable oil, for deep-frying

1 portion of Nordic Dill Salsa (page 120)

Historically, North Sea cod was—and still is—in big demand across northern and southern Europe thanks to its quality and flavour, but especially so in Catholic countries where fish has always been of great importance in their religious calendar. Poached, lightly salted cod with leek butter is one of the classic dishes of Norway. These spiced salt cod fritters are a fun, modern take on an old favourite.

*Melt* the butter in a small saucepan and add the flour, stirring continuously until the mixture looks golden and lumpy—you want to cook out the raw flour taste so hold your nerve and keep going for a minute or two. Remove the pan from the heat and add the milk. Stir again and put the milky-lumpy mixture back on the heat. Keep stirring over a low-medium heat while the mixture simmers for 2–3 minutes and thickens into a smooth sauce before removing from the heat.

Add the eggs, beating each one in with the whisk and then add the cod, anchovies, dill, allspice and pepper. This mixture can now be covered and kept in the fridge until needed.

When you're ready to make the fritters, heat the deep-fryer to 160°C, or heat oil in a large saucepan to the same temperature. Scoop tablespoonfuls of the salt cod mixture into the hot oil, about 4–6 at a time, and fry for 2 minutes on each side, or until each side is golden brown and evenly cooked. Remove from the oil with a large slotted spoon and drain on kitchen paper, then pop in a warm oven while you cook the rest. Serve warm with the Nordic Dill Salsa (or, if you prefer, a classic aïoli or tartar sauce would also go well).

# Hot Smoked Trout, Watercress, Pomegranate & Avocado Salad

Serves 6

Hot smoked trout earned the moniker 'Best Healthy Fast Food in the World' from my Anglo-American mother. She'd buy a whole hot smoked trout (a big one, not the puny little ones you often find) and serve it to guests with some sour cream alongside, pickled cucumber and crispbread. Healthy, delicious and ideal for a large gathering.

6 kiln-smoked rainbow trout fillets

200g watercress

seeds of 1 pomegranate

3 ripe avocados, chopped

zest and juice of 2 unwaxed lemons

handful of pumpkin seeds

assorted pickles (page 138)

1 small rye bread loaf (about 400g), thinly sliced and toasted in a low oven until completely dry to form chunky breadcrumbs

*Clean* the hot smoked trout of skin and any bones before flaking into bite-sized pieces. Divide the watercress between six plates and add the hot smoked trout pieces. Sprinkle over the pomegranate seeds, avocado, lemon zest and juice and pumpkin seeds, and add the assorted pickles before topping with the rye breadcrumbs.

# Smoked Chicken with Beets, Grains & Lentils

Chicken was always considered something of a luxury when I was growing up in Norway. Whole chickens were exorbitantly expensive so we never had the tradition of a chicken roast on Sundays like you have here in the UK. When I'm short on time, this is my go-to chicken dish—it's quick to prepare, full of diverse flavours and textures and supremely delicious.

Serves 4

*Rinse* the puy lentils and pearled spelt and cook according to the packet instructions (or use the ready-cooked variety if you're really famished and pressed for time). Once they're cooked, remove from the stove and allow to cool a little before assembling the salad.

Divide the ingredients equally between four plates, or arrange them on a large serving platter. Dress with the Nordic salsa, or a drizzle of oil and vinegar and some seasoning if you prefer to keep it simple. Scatter the herbs (if using), flowers and nuts around the dish to make a colourful arrangement and eat within an hour as the salad leaves and flowers will wilt quite quickly.

*Variations: As an alternative, try smoked duck or smoked venison, bacon, bresaola or any salty charcuterie/cured meat that complements the earthy flavour of the beets and the freshness of green herbs.*

200g puy lentils
200g pearled spelt (or barley)
400g smoked chicken, sliced
300g pickled beetroot, sliced
mixed salad of choice, washed and dried
1 portion of Nordic Dill Salsa (page 120)
	or oil and vinegar of your choice
salt and freshly ground black pepper

*To Serve*
1 bunch each of chervil, dill, parsley and
	chives (if you don't use the Nordic salsa)
edible flowers
toasted nuts such as pecans, hazelnuts,
	almonds and/or walnuts

# Spiced Roast Pork Belly

Christmas menus vary widely across Scandinavia; some parts of the region celebrate yule with seafood, others with a cold smörgåsbord. In parts of Norway, it's traditional to have *juleribbe* or roast pork, and this is my favourite way to cook pork belly. The aniseed flavour of fennel seeds and star anise really complement the piggy deliciousness, and allspice adds warmth and depth to this winter dish.

*Begin* the night before so the pork belly has a decent time to marinate. Using a Stanley knife or a very sharp chef's knife score the pork skin all the way down into the fat, taking care not to cut into the meat underneath. Place the pork in a large roasting tin and pour plenty of boiling water over the skin to puff it up—this helps the skin to crisp up during cooking. Drain the roasting tin of all the hot water and, using lots of kitchen paper, dry the skin and the flesh of the pork joint. A hairdryer is useful at this point, so if you have one handy then blow-dry the skin for 5–10 minutes. It makes all the difference in getting a good crackling so be patient with this step.

Next, crush the spices, salt and pepper in a pestle and mortar or in a small blender until they are finely blended. If you have any rough bits simply sieve them out so you're not chewing on crunchy spices when the pork is cooked.

In a small bowl mix the spiced salt with the honey and enough vegetable oil to bring the marinade together. Massage the marinade into the pork belly and make sure you get right into the crevices of the scored skin. Cover with cling film on a tray or keep in a large, sealed plastic food bag and refrigerate overnight.

The next day, when you're ready to roast the pork belly, preheat the oven to as high as it can go (240°C/

Serves 8–10

2kg pork belly
3 tbsp fennel seeds
1 tbsp allspice berries
2 star anise
1 tbsp coriander seeds
4 tbsp sea salt (or to your taste),
    plus extra for the crackling
1 tsp smoked sea salt (optional)
2 tbsp cracked black pepper
½ tsp white pepper
1 tbsp acacia honey
a little vegetable oil

*For the gravy (optional)*
brandy
chicken stock

gas mark 9 is fine). Place the pork belly in a large roasting tin and blast the skin again with the hairdryer for 5–10 minutes to really dry out the skin. Sprinkle a layer of sea salt over the skin before roasting—this helps with the crackling

Roast the pork belly in the hot oven for 15 minutes—the skin will start to crackle and pop so don't be alarmed if you hear some spitting noises from your oven. Open the oven door and turn down the temperature to 150°C/gas mark 2, pouring hot water into the roasting tin up to 1cm deep, to keep the pork meat moist and tender while cooking. Keep the oven door open until the oven temperature gauge shows it's reached 150°C—this will speed up the process of cooling the oven.

Roast for a further 2 hours. If you have time to really slow-roast the pork, reduce the oven to 130°C/gas mark ½ instead and roast for 3–4 hours for a really succulent result—but 2 hours at 150°C will produce a perfectly tender pork belly, too.

After the designated cooking time, remove the pork belly from the oven and give the crackling a tap. It should feel hard, but if it's still a little soft place the pork skin side down in a large frying pan and fry the crackling on a low-medium heat for 10–15 minutes. This should really seal the crackling. Allow to rest for 30 minutes before slicing and serving at your Christmas smörgåsbord.

In the meantime, remove three-quarters of the fat from the roasting tin, being careful not to drain away the meat juices from the pan. Make a jus or gravy if you wish, using a little brandy and some chicken stock to deglaze the pan. Keep warm until your guests arrive. Serve the pork with an assortment of your favourite salads, side dishes and pickles.

# Roast Rack of Lamb with a Rye, Herb & Spice Crust

**Rack of lamb is a really quick and delicious way of having roast lamb and this rye crust adds a little extra crunch and spice to the sweet lamb meat. A green salad on the side will cut through the richness of the lamb nicely. Any leftover lamb can be gnawed on the next day, or shorn from its rack and sliced into a salad or wrap.**

Serves 4

*Preheat* the oven to 190°C/gas mark 5.

Start by blitzing all the ingredients up to and including the white pepper in a blender so that you have an aromatic breadcrumb mixture.

Lightly season the lamb racks and place them fat side down in a hot pan with some oil, so you render and crisp the lamb fat before roasting the racks with the rye crumbs. Keep an eye on the lamb to make sure the fat doesn't burn. Place your lamb racks in a roasting dish so they stack against each other in two pairs. Allow them to cool slightly before using your hands to rub a little mustard over the surface of the racks. Press the breadcrumb mixture firmly on to the racks and put in the preheated oven—cook for 15 minutes if you like your lamb pink and 20–25 minutes if you like it a little more well done. Ovens vary so keep an eye on the racks as they cook.

When the lamb is done to your liking, remove from the oven and rest on a chopping board for 10–15 minutes before transferring to a large platter. Serve with a portion of the celeriac gratin on page 117 and an assortment of quick pickles such as fennel, cucumber and rhubarb (page 138).

125g rye breadcrumbs (see page 131) or panko breadcrumbs
30ml vegetable oil, plus extra for the pan
15g pack of flat-leaf parsley
15g pack of dill
2 Abba anchovy fillets (or 1 regular salty anchovy)
1 garlic clove, finely chopped
1 tsp French mustard, plus extra to rub on the lamb
1 tsp smoked sea salt
½ tsp freshly ground allspice
pinch of white pepper
4 x French-trimmed racks of lamb
salt and freshly ground black pepper

# PICKLES

The one taste I crave more than any other is tartness. When I was a toddler my mother was both bemused and somewhat horrified to discover that I absolutely loved lemons, and would happily chomp away on a cut lemon. At one point she wondered if I had a severe vitamin C deficiency but it turned out I was just a weird kid who loved sucking lemons.

Acidity can elevate a dish and I'm always drawn to cuisines that strike a balance between bold flavours, such as smoky, salty, spicy and sour. The tang of acidity is essential in the Scandinavian kitchen, and I'd wager that every single savoury dish in this book is improved when accompanied by a delicious, sour pickle.

# Quick Pickle Formula

This is a formula you can apply to any of the vegetables and fruits listed below. Simply scale it up if you need more for a large gathering but be aware that the quick pickle won't last more than 24 hours (in the case of cucumber it's really best eaten within a few hours).

*Pour* the vinegar into a small saucepan and add the caster sugar. Heat until the sugar dissolves completely but do not bring to the boil. Once the sugar has dissolved, remove the saucepan from the heat and allow to cool to lukewarm before adding thinly sliced cucumber (you can peel ribbons if you would like a different look to the cucumber pickle). Set aside and allow to pickle for 1 hour before using.

*Tip: The trick to a quick pickle is to slice the vegetable thinly and evenly so everything macerates at the same speed. You can make a coarser, crunchier quick pickle if you prefer, but you'll need to adjust the timing accordingly. Berries should be pickled whole.*

300ml white wine vinegar

150g caster sugar

1 cucumber, or equivalent weight in rhubarb, fennel, kohlrabi, celeriac, beetroot, carrot or berries such as blackberries

# Pickled
# Cherries

Makes enough to fill
a 1.5-litre glass jar

This makes a welcome change from cooking vast amounts of jam in the summer. Pickled cherries are tart, spicy and fruity, and make a perfect accompaniment to salads and game dishes. You can use small, seasonal plums as a variation if you wish, and the pickling liquor can also be used (in moderation) to jazz up salad dressings.

650g cherries
500ml red wine vinegar
200g fructose (fruit sugar)
3 allspice berries
3 cardamom pods
3 cloves
1 cinnamon stick
1 bay leaf
1 star anise
1 small knob of fresh ginger, crushed
1 long strip of lemon peel (from an
   unwaxed lemon if possible)

*Rinse* the cherries and, using a toothpick, pierce each one a few times (this allows the pickle to permeate the cherries)—you may want to co-opt children or friends to help you with this time-consuming task! Place the pricked cherries in a sterilized glass container large enough to hold the pickling liquid, or several smaller glass containers instead.

In a saucepan bring the vinegar, sugar, spices, lemon peel and 200ml water to the boil and simmer for 5 minutes to allow the spices to infuse.

Pour the pickling solution over the cherries and cover with a lid. Allow to cool completely before placing in the fridge. The pickled cherries are best when left unopened for at least 2 weeks or more so that the flavour develops fully. They are delicious with cured venison, in salads or just to munch on their own.

Remember to tell everyone that the stones are still in the cherries, to avoid any expensive trips to the dentist!

six

—

healthy

hedonism

# ———— Skål!

It's often said that we Nordics live in a state of healthy hedonism, and pride ourselves on keeping a sense of perspective on life. That applies not only to our food culture but to our enjoyment of alcohol too. We love a tipple. Sometimes the narrative about the Nordic region can convey a certain puritanical streak, but I reckon it's our love of alcohol that helps to maintain hygge all year round.

Singing is also essential to this sense of conviviality and good times. We love to drink and sing at special occasions, which can be a little daunting to foreign visitors unfamiliar with our customs, especially those who have never been to a Nordic wedding, when the singing is prolific.

The hygge approach to alcohol is decidedly *not* about getting drunk, and it doesn't really involve spending an evening in a pub or binge-drinking. I learnt at a young age that alcohol wasn't about inebriation, but about flavour. That's why I love whisky so much. You may prefer gin or brandy, as is your prerogative. In the Nordic region, there's no such thing as a 'man's drink', so when I first arrived to study at university here in the UK I found the notion that women weren't supposed to drink beer or whisky a little peculiar to say the least. To my mind if a drink is served in a beautiful glass, who cares what people think?

This chapter covers all my favourites: winter warmers, a rum-based flip to recall the Norse goddess Freya and a refreshing summer punch to celebrate midsummer. As always, alcohol is best served with delicious food, so try making the Allspice & Whisky Chicken Skewers on page 109 or the Spiced Salt Cod Fritters on page 129 to go alongside these drinks. If you're in a celebratory mood, why not make the malty hot chocolate and have that with a Dark Chocolate Muffin (see page 75)? Or take it easy and just raid the salted nuts and potato crisps section of your local store—there's no need to be precious when it comes to alcohol-enhanced hygge. This is about conviviality, cosiness and the fun you can have creating simple cocktails at home …

# Triple
# Cherry Gløgg

Serves 10 in heatproof
glasses or cups

Cherries have a particular resonance. They remind me of summers spent at my grandparents' fruit farm on the west coast of Norway. I can conjure up their intense flavour even on the darkest of midwinter days, and I enjoy nothing more than sharing that experience with friends and family with a glass of this Triple Cherry Gløgg—it's dark, rich, sweet and sour all at the same time.

*For the Spiced Sugar Syrup*

100g golden caster sugar

10 cardamom pods, crushed

5 whole cloves

3 peppercorns

3 star anise

1 cinnamon stick

1cm piece of fresh ginger

1 long strip of unwaxed clementine rind
   (or citrus peel of your choice)

*For the Cherries*

150ml cherry cordial

150ml cherry liqueur such as Cherry Heering

100g dried sour cherries

75cl bottle of light red wine
   such as Beaujolais

*To Serve*

2 organic clementines,
   peeled and sliced into discs

100g blanched almonds

To make the spiced sugar syrup, heat the sugar in a small saucepan with 100ml water. Turn off the heat as soon as the sugar has dissolved. Add all the spices and the citrus peel, cover and allow to infuse overnight or for at least a few hours.

Do the same with the cherries (but without heating them). Place all the ingredients in a bowl and leave covered overnight.

When you're ready to serve the gløgg, place the syrup and cherries in a large pan and heat gently. You do not want to boil this under any circumstances. It should be just hot enough so there is a little steam coming off the liquid but nothing more. I like to leave it on a low heat like this for about 20 minutes so all the flavours infuse together. Place one or two clementine slices in each glass or cup along with a couple of almonds and then carefully ladle in some of the gløgg. Serve while warm.

*Tip: It's definitely worth making a large batch of spiced sugar syrup as it features in other recipes in this chapter, so double or triple the quantities for the syrup and keep what you don't use for the gløgg in the fridge in a sealed, sterilized glass container for up to 3 weeks.*

# Hot Christmas

Cayenne pepper adds a lip-tingling heat to this drink—essentially it's a riff on the classic yuletide hot buttered rum. Much like when cooking, it's important to taste as you go along so that you don't overdo the cayenne. The trick is to get enough of it stirred in so you feel that tingling sensation but you don't blow the roof off and spend hours wheezing, crying and coughing. Nothing hot about that at all ...

*Divide* the butter and maple syrup between the glasses or cups. Add the spices and seasoning, then pour in the rum. Top up with boiling water and whisk gently so that the butter emulsifies with the rum. Check to see if there's enough heat and spice, and adjust according to your own taste. Add the cinnamon sticks, if using, and serve immediately.

Serves 2 in heatproof glasses or cups

50g butter

2 tbsp maple syrup (or Spiced Sugar Syrup, page 143, if you prefer)

pinch each of cayenne pepper, cinnamon, nutmeg and vanilla sea salt

120ml golden rum (I use The Duppy Share, but any good golden rum will do)

hot water from the kettle

2 cinnamon sticks (optional)

∞

From top: *Triple Cherry Gløgg* (page 143); *Hot Christmas*

# Sizzling
# January

We don't really see the point of 'dryanuary' or any of that spurious detox nonsense. The month of January is a time to embrace the reality of being a little bit broke, while carrying on the festive indoor hygge of midwinter with bright candles, good food, drink and company. This twist on a whisky hot toddy is the perfect après-ski (or any outdoor activity) cocktail, guaranteed to turn this bleakest of months into a sizzling one.

*Simply* mix everything in a heatproof jug, adding hot water to taste (and according to how hot you like your drink—I like it piping hot but not everyone does). You can play around with the strength of the drink according to your own taste. Feel free to use rum instead of whisky, and try replacing the hot water with a tea such as Lady Grey if you wish.

Serves 2 in heatproof
glasses or cups

80ml (or 2 shots) mild whisky
2 tbsp cherry liqueur
    such as Cherry Heering
4 tbsp Spiced Sugar Syrup (page 143)
4 dashes of cardamom bitters
2 slices of blood orange (with peel)
pinch of vanilla salt
hot water from the kettle

# Boozy, Malty, Creamy Hot Chocolate

Serves 1 in a heatproof
glass or cup

I made this for Papa Johansen, who declared it the best hot chocolate ever. Well, he would say that, but I hope you'll agree. No one will blame you if you make this just for yourself, but it's so good that you'll want to share it.

2 tbsp Ovaltine

25–50ml (1–2 shots) whisky

150ml whole milk

20g dark chocolate

1 tbsp good cocoa powder,
    plus extra for dusting

pinch of vanilla salt

dollop of double cream

ground cinnamon, for dusting

*Place* the Ovaltine and whisky in the heatproof glass or cup and stir slightly so you have a paste. In a small saucepan warm the milk with the dark chocolate, cocoa powder and vanilla salt. Using a small whisk, stir over a medium heat until the hot chocolate looks even and starts to steam. Once it looks molten and delicious, pour a little into the glass with the Ovaltine and whisky, stir, and then pour in the remainder of the hot chocolate mixture. Scoop a dollop of double cream on top and dust with a little extra cocoa powder and some cinnamon before slurping away. That's hygge in a mug right there!

"*This is about conviviality, and the fun you can have creating cocktails at home.*" ——

# Spiced
# Clementine Sour

Serves 1

We're fans of a whisky sour in this household, and this is a gentle riff on a true whisky sour, with aromatic clementine and a little contrasting spice from the spiced sugar syrup.

50ml whisky

20ml fresh clementine juice

20ml Spiced Sugar Syrup (page 143)

20ml fresh lemon juice

1 egg white

small handful of ice

*To Serve*

a few dashes of The Bitter
   Truth Lemon Bitters

freshly grated zest of 1 unwaxed clementine

dusting of ground cinnamon

*Chill* the tumbler or sour glass you intend to serve this in—the colder, the better.

Next place all the ingredients excluding the ice in a cocktail shaker and shake for a few seconds. Open the shaker and add a decent amount of ice. Seal with the lid again and shake for a few more seconds until it's very cold.

Strain the clementine sour into your chilled glass, add a couple of dashes of lemon bitters, a sprinkling of freshly grated clementine zest along with a dusting of cinnamon and drink immediately.

# Champagne
# & Haribo Candy

Serves 6

At the risk of you thinking I'm a complete dilettante, let me just say that not only is this drink tremendous fun to serve, but you can of course use other sparkling wine. Champagne and Haribo just has a nice ring to it and, as with most cocktails, came about more by accident than design—I had an abundance of Haribo left over from a party and a mini bottle of champagne in the fridge ... well, it had to be tried!

180 ml peach liqueur

Haribo of choice (I like a mix of gummy bears and Tangfastics)

75cl bottle of sparkling wine, cava or Prosecco of choice (or champagne if you're feeling flush)

*Pour* 30ml of the peach liqueur in each of six champagne flutes and add the Haribo—one or two of each type. Top up with fizz and stir a little so the Haribo start to bob and dance about. Drink. And watch out for those tipsy Haribo—they're the best part.

# Freya's Flip

Flips are essentially a combination of a spirit, a whole egg, some sugar, spices and maybe a splash of cream. Served hot or cold, they are absolutely delicious. Given the Norse goddess Freya's mythological status as a wielder of magic, I've dedicated this to her. Freya's frothy, creamy concoction is given a modern twist by using almond milk and adding cardamom and cocoa bitters. It's like a boozy dessert, and who doesn't love that?

Serves 1

*Chill* a sour glass, tumbler or a martini/coupette glass so it's ready for the flip.

Place all the ingredients except the ice, cardamom and cocoa nibs in a cocktail shaker. Shake well for a few seconds to mix everything together. Add a good amount of ice, seal the shaker again and shake until very cold.

Strain the flip into the chilled glass then dust with ground cardamom and sprinkle a few cocoa nibs on top of the froth. Drink immediately.

60ml unsweetened almond milk
  (I use Rude Health's Ultimate Almond)
40ml golden rum
20ml Spiced Sugar Syrup (page 143)
1 whole egg
a few dashes of cardamom bitters
a few dashes of cocoa bitters
pinch of sea salt
ice
ground cardamom and cocoa nibs,
  to decorate

∞

**Left to right:** *Fruits of the Forest Punch* (page 155); *Skadi's Spritz* (page 154); *Freya's Flip*

# Skadi's Spritz

Skadi was a Norse goddess tormentor, most famously of Loki. She hunted, was a winter maven of sorts and generally evinced a certain 'don't mess with me' attitude that we could all probably do with channelling. Given Skadi's badass reputation, I thought it fitting to pay tribute to her with this complex, bitter, woodsy, sour, salty and sweet spritz—a grapefruit bombshell of a drink. Get a group of spirited women together and toast Skadi with them ...

*Start* by making a grapefruit and thyme salt: in a bowl place a handful of sea salt and the zest of half the grapefruit along with a few leaves from the thyme sprigs. Mix together (use your hands if you like) until you have a fragrant citrus-thyme salt. If necessary, add more citrus and thyme.

Slice the zested grapefruit in half and press gently into the rim of the glass, then dip the glass into the salt (repeat if you're making more than one spritz).

Next squeeze 50ml juice from the zested grapefruit half and pour into the glass with the vodka, sugar syrup, lemon juice, Campari and grapefruit bitters. Add a few cubes of ice and a sprig of thyme to the glass before stirring and then topping up with sparkling water. Serve with a wedge of pink grapefruit, cut from the unzested half, as an extra garnish and drink.

Serves 1

sea salt
1 pink grapefruit
a few sprigs of thyme
40ml vodka
20ml Spiced Sugar Syrup (page 143)
   or simple sugar syrup, if you prefer
10ml fresh lemon juice
5ml Campari
a few dashes of grapefruit bitters
ice cubes
sparkling water, to top up

# Fruits of the
# Forest Punch

Serves 6–8

A good punch is really underrated, and that's a pity as it's so easy to make for a large crowd. This is my midsummer punch, replete with delicious northern European berries and a gentle spice from the sugar syrup from the cherry gløgg recipe on page 143. Skål!

75cl bottle of light red wine such as
   Beaujolais or a darker rosé wine
250ml cherry liqueur
   such as Cherry Heering
250ml blueberry juice
150ml fresh lemon juice
100ml vodka, gin or aquavit
100ml Spiced Sugar Syrup (page 143)
a few dashes each of cherry,
   cardamom and citrus bitters
handful each of fresh blueberries, cherries,
   raspberries, strawberries and redcurrants
cinnamon sticks and whole star anise
lemon slices

*To Serve*
ice cubes
600ml sparkling water

*Place* all the ingredients in a large punch bowl and give everything a good stir.

Taste the punch and see if it's to your liking. Add more of any of the ingredients if you feel it needs a little extra oomph, bearing in mind that you will dilute the flavour somewhat when you add ice and sparkling water.

When you're ready to serve the punch, add the ice and sparkling water, and let your guests help themselves.

# Scandinavian Summer Punch

Serves 6–8

A delicious alternative to the sickly sweet summer cocktails you often find at garden parties and picnics, this summer cup is as cool as a cucumber and easy to prepare. Serve chilled in tall glasses, and the longer you leave the lemons, cucumber and mint to macerate, the better this drink will taste. Summer berries such as blueberries or white currants look pretty as a garnish but are not essential.

1.5 litres sparkling water

green tea leaves or bags
   (I use Rare Tea Company green tea)

300ml vodka

150ml elderflower cordial, or more
   according to your taste

2 lemons, sliced into discs

1 cucumber, chopped or sliced into sticks
   for swirling the drink in your glass

1 bunch of mint leaves

ice cubes, to serve (optional)

*A* few hours before you're going to serve this, infuse the sparkling water with the green tea and make sure to seal the bottle well so you don't lose too many bubbles. If you use loose tea, remember to strain the leaves out before assembling the cocktail. Keep the sparkling water in the fridge until you're ready to roll.

In a large pitcher or punch bowl mix the vodka, elderflower cordial and all the remaining ingredients. Blend together with the green tea-infused sparkling water, cover and place in the fridge for about 1 hour. You can serve it immediately but the macerating ingredients do really lift this drink.

Serve as is, or over ice for extra refreshment.

seven
———
design
& home

# Keep it Simple

'Simplicity is the ultimate sophistication.'

Steve Jobs

At the heart of this book is the belief that if you have a roof over your head, a table to gather round with friends and loved ones, some delicious food and maybe a glass to hand, then all you need is time spent in nature and you've got it made. We Nordics are as contented being homebodies as we are exploring the great outdoors, and that balance really is the key to understanding our way of life. In essence, the world of Nordic hygge is about getting back to basics, about simplifying your life. After all, why overcomplicate everything during your brief time on this planet when simplicity is the foundation of good living?

In recent years I've found myself heeding Henry David Thoreau's words more and more:

'Our life is frittered away by detail. An honest man has hardly need to count more than his ten fingers or in extreme cases he may add his ten toes, and lump the rest. Simplicity, simplicity, simplicity! I say, let your affairs be as two or three, and not a hundred or a thousand; instead of a million count half a dozen, and keep your accounts on your thumb nail. In the midst of this chopping sea of civilized life, such are the clouds and storms and quicksands and thousand-and-one items to be allowed for, that a man has to live, if he would not founder and go to the bottom and not make his port at all, by dead reckoning, and he must be a great calculator indeed who succeeds. Simplify, simplify. Instead of three meals a day, if it be necessary eat but one; instead of a hundred dishes, five; and reduce other things in proportion.'

— Henry David Thoreau, *Walden or, Life in the Woods*, 1854

Our lives really are frittered away by detail. Paring everything back to a few timeless essentials means we can be freed from the relentless pressure to consume, to be the best, to stay in fashion—to keep up with the exhausting merry-go-round of modern living. The truth is none of it matters. Simplicity, simplicity, simplicity!

That is the heart of hygge.

But what does all this mean in the context of Nordic design and creating a beautiful home? Some of you reading this may already be familiar with the beautiful objects made in the frozen North. Arne Jacobsen's 'Egg' chair, for example, became famous in the UK thanks to its role as the seat in the confessional diary room during the first season of *Big Brother* (or so I'm told; it's not a programme I have any real affinity for).

Originally designed in 1958 for the Radisson SAS hotel in Copenhagen and now made by Danish furniture design company Republic of Fritz Hansen, the 'Egg' is but one in a collection of memorable chairs in the Nordic design catalogue. In fact, we're rather fond of great chair design; pretty much every notable Nordic designer came up with their own characteristic spin on this humble item of furniture. Another Nordic chair of note was the 'Round' one designed by Hans Wegner—those with a keen eye for history may know it better as the chair John F. Kennedy sat in for the first live televised presidential debate with Richard Nixon back in 1960. When I asked Max Fraser, founder and editor of *London Design Guide* (londondesignguide.com), which object of Nordic design he would consider investing in, he replied: 'I would go for the PK22 chair [by Poul Kjaerholm for Fritz Hansen] in leather. It's so elegant, comfortable and true to its form, and the leather ages beautifully over time. My dad owns one that I will hopefully inherit one day, with battered old leather!' Beautiful, timeless design that is made to last: themes that recur as we take a closer look at Nordic design ...

Perhaps you've been smitten by the craft and textiles of the Nordic region? Mention the 'Sarah Lund jumper' (also known as '*The Killing* jumper', which sounds less benign) to a certain kind of Nordic noir fan and they'll immediately enthuse about how much they adore Gudrun & Gudrun's patterns. My supper club partner Hannah and I once hosted a brunch to mark the series finale of *The Killing*, and asked our guests to come wearing their favourite jumper. One guest arrived wearing the same one made famous by Sofie Gråbøl in the TV programme, only to be upstaged by a fellow guest who had knitted her own version of the pattern! They looked identical, but the prize of the day unquestionably went to the one who dedicated herself to so many hours of knitting. As for my own jumper wardrobe, I have a Dale sweater made in western Norway that I've owned since the mid-1990s which could reasonably be classified as vintage (it's featured on page 20), but my most prized jumper possession is the one Grandma Johansen knitted for my father back in the 1960s before he left for college in the US. Still in mint condition, this classic Norwegian 'Mariusgenser' pattern is a family heirloom to treasure in years to come.

Those interested in architecture may already be familiar with Finnish designer Alvar Aalto's magnificent buildings such as Villa Mairea, a retreat built in Noormarkku in 1939, or his earlier work on the Paimio tuberculosis sanatorium, completed in 1932. Described by *Architectural Digest* as one of the 'most impressive buildings of the 20th century', this beacon of Nordic architecture was designed with the purpose of healing at its core.

Bibliophiles hold Swedish designer Gunnar Asplund's Stockholm Public Library in high esteem; indeed, his building is often cited in lists of the world's top libraries. A pivotal figure in the surge of creativity in Sweden that catapulted the region into international recognition in the 1920s, Asplund is also closely associated with the Stockholm International Exhibition in 1930, which helped to catapult Nordic design into a region-wide movement.

# Swedish Grace

*'Beautiful home surroundings would be sure to make people happier.'*
—          Ellen Key, *'Skönhet för Alla'* ('Beauty for All'), 1899

'Swedish Grace', a phrase coined by Philip Morton Shand, the British architecture critic, journalist and food/drink writer, described the Nordic designs featured at the 1925 Exposition Internationale des Arts Décoratifs in Paris. It was a seminal moment in the story of twentieth-century Nordic design, one cited by the co-founder of Skandium, Magnus Englund, in his forthcoming book on the history of this subject. Ellen Key, a widely published and translated Swedish writer at the turn of the twentieth century, had a profound influence on this movement which was to evolve in subsequent years. Her argument still resonates today with anyone who grew up in the region: the 'beautiful is that which is practical, useful, informed by its purpose, and expressive of the soul of its user or creator'. Beauty started in the *home*, and Key believed that everyone had the potential to create an aesthetically pleasing domestic space, and in doing so they would transform their lives. If you can be happy at home, society as a whole will benefit, Key argued. It may seem Pollyannaish but I reckon she was on to something, and her enlightened belief in the positive power of a beautiful home is one to which we Nordics still subscribe.

Furthermore, Key believed it was possible to design a beautiful, domestic aesthetic and that it was a fundamental right of every person. Good design was decidedly *not* the preserve of an elite. Swedish artist Carl Larsson, a contemporary of Ellen Key, published *Ett Hem* (1899), a book that would have an equally profound effect on the culture of Nordic design for many decades to come. Larsson's cosy illustrations became a visual primer for the modern Nordic aesthetic, and while they may look quaint today, they proved influential with their message of economy, simplicity and warmth in the home—aspirations all Nordics grow up with, and which everyone can achieve with a little effort. Sweden, in particular, became synonymous with progressive policies throughout the twentieth

*"The world of Nordic hygge is about getting back to basics, about simplifying your life."* ———

century, with design and social democratic policies integrating in later years, echoing Ellen Key's assertion that beauty in design could have a profound effect on society at large. 'Democratic by design' is how Andrew Graham-Dixon described Sweden's art and design in his BBC television programme *Art of Scandinavia*, and thanks to IKEA we all probably recognize some aspect of that accessibility of Nordic design. Love them or hate them, IKEA have successfully spread this visual language to a global audience, with a philosophy anchored in pragmatic concerns about the way people live that can be traced back to those early twentieth-century Swedish designers and artists.

# Design is Refined to its Essence

Thanks to those long, dark winters, people have historically adapted quite well to the harsh climate of the North by making solid cabins or houses designed to protect us from howling winds, icy snow storms and the occasional attack by a ravenous bear. There is a robustness to our buildings; they're fit for purpose and reflect a certain toughness, a rigour, and the no-nonsense attitude of those living in the region. As Elizabeth Wilhide writes in *Scandinavian Modern Home*:

*'To survive in such inhospitable conditions, over the centuries Scandinavians have developed a strong practical bent that makes the most out of limited resources and delivers workable solutions with optimum economy. When materials are in short supply, they must be used as efficiently as possible and minimisation of waste became as much a part of Scandinavian traditions of craft as a common-sense approach to problem-solving. Before the modernists' credo "form follows function" was ever coined, the useful everyday objects produced by Scandinavian craftworkers displayed such a conviction.'*

Nowadays double-glazed windows are standard, underfloor heating is almost seen as a human right thanks to our modern deployment of ancient hypocaust technology that allows us to walk around barefoot in winter (take that, carpets!), and we use the materials available in our surroundings to create hygge in our homes, all year long.

∞

A pared-back home aesthetic is accessible whatever your budget

That Nature sets the pace in the Nordic region has been a recurring theme in this book, and our design traditions are deeply rooted in nature and the timeless aesthetic of the outdoors, the landscape and the seasons. Indeed, when I asked Kai Price and Amanda Nelson, founders of online Nordic interiors store Att Pynta (attpynta.com), why so many people outside the region are drawn to Nordic design, their reply came as no surprise:

*'There is a timeless element to the Nordic aesthetic as often it features clean lines and feels contemporary. Nordic design is often focused around functionality rather than just the way it looks alone, which we think resonates with people. Because function is at the heart of Nordic design it rarely feels outdated. The Nordic aesthetic is a look that can easily be updated by adding or taking away pieces but still keeping the overall Nordic feel.'*

It's that lack of pretension, and focus on stylish but practical items, which channels Finnish designer Alvar Aalto's dictum that 'Beauty is the harmony of purpose and form'—the Nordic design aesthetic in a nutshell.

Good design is deeply embedded in our history, and our sense of who we are. Ask any Finnish child to name the country's most famous architect and designer and they'll answer, without hesitation, 'Alvar Aalto'. After all, Aalto's work is widely recognized as among the twentieth century's greatest, right up there with Le Corbusier. 'As a rule of thumb,' Magnus Englund told me, 'Finnish design is at one end of the spectrum and Danish design is at the other, with Sweden closer to the Finnish aesthetic and Norway closer to Denmark.' As Magnus explained, Finland's design heritage is regarded as the more esoteric end of the spectrum, and Denmark's is considered the more accessible. That's a deliberate generalization, of course, and there are exceptions, but if you're curious about the more avant-garde side of Nordic design then Finland is a good place to start.

While researching this subject, I noticed certain tropes emerging in the media coverage and literature on the appeal of Nordic interiors. Design aficionados the world over wax lyrical about Nordic designers. I asked Max Fraser what he found so compelling about our design culture:

—— *"We use the materials available in our surroundings to create hygge in our homes."*

'There are a number of compelling aspects: one is the lack of superfluous detailing, concerned as they are with functionality and clean silhouettes. There is also a respect for materials with an emphasis on natural and tactile materials like wood. Designs tend to be confident yet understated, even if they embrace bold colours or forms. Design is refined to its essence.'

In sum, if you're new to Nordic design here are some useful crib notes:

# Nordic Design is ...

∞ Functional, yet stylish—a reflection of the pragmatism of both designers and people in the region
∞ Contrasting colours and textures that work in harmony with each other
∞ Minimalist, yet warm
∞ Focused on natural materials: wood, stone, fur, wool and glass
∞ Inspired by organic forms: lakes, fjords, mountains, waterfalls, forests, sea, ice, fire
∞ Accessible and—often, but not always—affordable
∞ Uses light in various forms to add a bright cosiness
∞ Prioritizes quality craftsmanship over mediocrity
∞ A mix of old and new
∞ Anchored in a democratic spirit in which design is deemed vital to everyone's quality of life
∞ And as a consequence perhaps of that last characteristic: shuns overly ostentatious designs and displays of conspicuous consumption

As we have already seen, the spirit of self-reliance and looking to nature for inspiration is central to Nordic identity. These qualities resonate with many who are disillusioned with a throwaway consumer culture. In an age of austerity, we've seen a surge in upcycling thanks to a 'make do and mend' spirit channelling our grandparents' generation and their thriftiness. Instagram and Pinterest abound with images of clever design hacks that require little more than ingenuity and elbow grease. It seems many of us want to make and do things with *meaning*, not to squander the few resources we have available.

# How to Hygge at Home

*'Don't own so much clutter that you will be relieved
to see your house catch fire.'*

—
Wendell Berry

So how can you create hygge at home? You're looking for a space that gives you a sense of warmth and calm when you walk through it, and lures you to a cosy spot to enjoy—you guessed it—that slice of cake basking in the soft glow of flickering candles. It's a home that is inviting, one that absolutely does *not* have to be big, fancy or ostentatious in its decor. As we've already established, the Nordic design ethos is characterized by a lack of pretension, and displays of conspicuous consumption are somewhat frowned upon. Hygge can be created in the smallest of spaces, so whether you share a flat, or a tiny studio, you can create hygge wherever you are. The key is to look at your surroundings with an open mind, and a realistic vision of how it should look that fits within your budget.

The first step to achieving this is to critically assess your interior space:

Do you feel calm and contented with your lot when you spend a period of time at home? If not, take a look around you: is it full of clutter and stuff that's accumulated over the years without any rhyme or reason? Wendell Berry's words about clutter make eminent sense—we can all probably do with hoarding less stuff.

When were the rooms last painted? Are the windows dirty? Do you see much natural light coming in?

The next step is, of course, to give your place a thorough spring-clean. Or an autumn-clean. In fact, a major clean at any time of the year will do the trick, even if you're not dramatically changing your living space. We Nordics are fastidious about tidy spaces: as the saying goes, 'a tidy space equals a tidy mind', but from an aesthetic standpoint, clutter and mess simply aren't beautiful. You don't have to be militant about keeping everything *just so*; the idea of this book is to bring a little everyday hygge into your life, not to trigger a full-blown obsessive-compulsive tidying frenzy that sends you into a complete meltdown.

I know it can seem a drag in theory, but a little effort in keeping on top of the domestic jumble is really worth your time. As mentioned in earlier chapters, to be active is to be alive, and that applies not just to your health and fitness, but to keeping your home as hygge as possible. If your interior space is messy, there's mould in various spots and the atmosphere is dark and drab, you'll feel glum spending your precious free time there. When I've had a thorough tidy of our household I get a thrill like Doris Day in *Calamity Jane* when she converts her dusty cabin into a small sanctuary of domestic charm and cosiness. A little effort can result in a great deal of joy. A beautiful home is one that allows you to feel protected and safe—who doesn't want that?

Make cleaning a social occasion—seriously! Get your family and/or friends together one weekend, bribe them with the promise of food and drink and make the cleaning of your home a co *lective* effort. When I was growing up in Norway all the neighbours near us came together every spring and had a *dugnad*, which was a communal spring-clean of the neighbourhood. It's not necessarily altruism at work; everyone gains from the joint effort of sprucing up the area—we all benefit from living some- where that looks like a little care and effort has gone into maintaining it. Hygge is as much about community and togetherness as it is about creat- ing your own beautiful home.

The tradition of *dugnad* reminds me of French anthropologist and sociologist Marcel Mauss's seminal text *The Gift*, in which he cites the *Hávamál*, one of the oldest poems of the Norse *Edda*, to introduce the topic of how central reciprocal exchange was to social solidarity. As humans are social animals, this cycle of reciprocity is fundamental to social relations. Offer to reciprocate when others are contemplating a big tidying operation in their home, or indeed neighbourhood. It's a gesture that goes a long way to maintaining good relationships with those you love, and of course a good deed is a reward in itself. Not only will the time fly but working as a small team means you'll gain new perspectives on your interior space.

Once you've cleared your flat or house of any unnecessary clutter, old paperwork and miscellaneous junk that no one is using anymore, step back and have a think about which pieces of furniture, accessories, lamps, etc. are the ones you really want to amplify. Which should take pride of place, which complement each other? You might find items that were previously tucked away, or that have some meaning, or discover that the knick-knack you inherited from an eccentric aunt suddenly looks more attractive than you thought. Or the pieces might even simply look better without a blanket of dust. Then assess the surrounding walls. Are they complementing these lovely things you have, or does everything look a little tired?

It doesn't take much to revive a room, and you don't have to go down the route of painting everything white either, an oft-cited cliché of how to make an interior space more Nordic. To my mind, a house full of white walls is reminiscent of a sanatorium but some people absolutely love all-white interiors and find them soothing. If you find white walls sterile, try contrasting colours with wood, such as shades of grey, pale blues and greens and even an off-beat colour like pale pink or yellow (the latter is especially warm in children's rooms, projecting a sense of sunny optimism). Think about what colours make you feel calm and happy, how those colours work with the items you own (or plan to purchase) and then plan a scheme for each room accordingly. It's always better to spend time thinking through what you want to achieve with your home, than to randomly acquire new objects without rhyme or reason.

# Banish that Carpet

To anyone who grew up in the Nordic region, the idea of putting carpet on your lovely floors is bananas. Loco. I mean, it's mind-boggling on so many levels. Why carpets are cherished in other countries is an enduring mystery to us, right up there with the ending of *Twin Peaks*.

If it were up to me I would rip up carpets from every home and make a bonfire to end all bonfires. Think about it: dust, dirt, dander, bacteria, mould and mildew all become deeply embedded in carpets, and unless you rigorously vacuum and frequently deep-clean them (and, be honest, how many people actually do this?) then they are simply *infested*. There's no tiptoeing around this: to us Nordics carpets are utterly disgusting. You might be thinking, 'But a little bit of dirt is good for you!' Yes, getting your hands dirty when potting plants is good for you, as is the daily exposure we have to other human beings—there are lots of useful ways to boost your immune system. I'm well versed in the literature on good bacteria and the science of the human microbiome, but if you want to have an authentically Nordic home of hygge then the mantra 'cleanliness is next to godliness' really is essential, and that means floors which can be properly cleaned with soap and water. 'But I love the feel of carpet on my feet' is another answer I get when I raise the issue of how much we loathe carpets. To which my response is: put on a pair of socks and get yourself a comfy pair of (quiet) slippers. We also find the idea of wearing outdoor shoes around a home completely baffling. They're to be left in the entrance. Bringing your outdoor shoes into a Nordic home is an act of defilement deemed the equivalent of going into a field, picking up a cow pat and using it as a Frisbee thrown across someone's home, spraying manure everywhere.

∞
Wooden floors are cherished across the Nordic region: why would you cover your home with the dirt magnet known as carpet?

If you really can't stand the idea of a bare floor made of wood, tile or stone then a few rugs and animal skins add warmth and texture to any living space. But whatever you do, if you have the option—and I appreciate this isn't always the case when renting—banish that carpet.

Thinking about how to create a hygge home made me realize how lucky I was growing up in Norway (aside from the fact that our homes never had the dreaded carpet). We were surrounded by simple, good design, well-built houses and buildings, and everything looked clean, light and fresh. Our home had wooden floors, a bathroom with underfloor heated tiles to keep toes cosy and warm in the winter months, and we even had a small sauna to sweat out any tension from everyday life after a busy week, or to revive ourselves after a day's cross-country skiing. Heating was never an issue as we had a Swedish 'kake'ugn', commonly known as a 'kachelöfen'— a stove covered in white tiles on the middle floor of the house that was so

—— *"A hygge home is one that gives you a sense of warmth and calm."*

efficient in radiating heat from a few logs of wood that we never worried about heating bills. Our house was built into a mountainside, so there was no terrain on which to create a garden. Instead, my parents constructed a rock garden with alpine flowers and herbs. We just made the best of our environment, rather than fighting it.

In order to give you the best how-to-hygge-at-home tips, I asked Kai and Amanda of Att Pynta, Max Fraser and Magnus Englund from Skandium to share their expertise in what to look for if you're thinking of redecorating your home in a Nordic way. Here's their advice:

# Let There Be Light

*'It doesn't cost money to light a room correctly,*
*but it does require culture.'*

—                                                        Poul Henningsen

According to Kai and Amanda, if you would like to add a real sense of hygge to your home, 'Go for several small light sources (ideally with a dimmer)

when lighting your home in the evening rather than one bright light. This will instantly create a calm and relaxing mood in your home. We've found that our vintage bulbs with the dimmer plug have been very popular for creating that look.' Viewers of cult Danish TV series *Borgen* may already be familiar with the 'Artichoke' lamp designed by Poul Henningsen for Louis Poulsen in 1958—without a doubt the most famous pendant light in Nordic design. It's a magnificent lighting statement, but thanks to the expert craftsmanship and skill involved in its manufacture it's not cheap. Think of this as an investment piece to save up for. Yet Henningsen maintained that you didn't have to spend a lot of money in order to light a room properly. Design magazines, websites and blogs will give you plenty of inspiration if you want something a little off-piste; but the main thing to remember is to have a variety of lights, in different strengths and with perhaps an unusual lampshade or two to add a little texture to a room.

# You Can Never Have Too Many Candles

I've been somewhat dismissive of the 'hygge is cosy candles' cliché, but truth be told candles do make a difference, especially in the dark winter months. We light them often, and without an occasion to justify it. I light candles when I'm working at my desk, when I've cooked a meal, when I'm reading, or when I'm in the bath. It's that added warmth you get from candlelight (especially if you don't have a fireplace or stove oven) which is essential when it's miserable outside. Lit candles are a failsafe way to cheer a gloomy room. Opt for a few simple candle holders, sparkling votives (I'm partial to the ones made by Iittala and they're not exorbitant in price) and have a few different shapes and sizes too. Whatever you do, don't leave lit tea lights naked on surfaces at waist height otherwise you might find your dress on fire, as happened to me once at a party. Protect your candles, protect your clothing ...

# Plant Hygge

Danish architect and designer Arne Jacobsen was a keen gardener and often incorporated plants into his designs. Now that you've cracked the

∞
Architectural plants such as succulents look great and are so easy to maintain

lighting situation, bring nature indoors. That indoor/outdoor juxtaposition is one that has been used to great effect, and many buildings are designed with the intention of bringing the natural world inside. Pop to your local florist or garden centre, or head online to buy as many plants as you can afford. Architectural plants, succulents in particular, add a certain flair to any room no matter what its size or shape, and they are so easy to maintain. Make sure you stick to the rule of odd numbers when displaying plants (the same goes for votives) and dust them regularly. You can upcycle old plant pots by painting them in different colours, even adding a little metallic shine with copper or silver glass paint if you have the time and inclination.

As Kai and Amanda also suggest, getting a stylish vase in a colour you love will make cut flowers look more like a statement, and when the vase is empty you can display it as an elegant ornament in itself. The classic 'paper bag vase' designed by Tapio Wirkkala for Rosenthal in 1977 still looks fresh today. You don't have to go down the route of investing in a design classic when it comes to vases but scour Pinterest, Instagram and design sites for unusual statement vases and find one you like which is within your price bracket. If you can afford a couple more in different shapes and sizes then they make a stylish display together but one is plenty. Both sides of my family are keen gardeners and lovers of plants, flowers and wildlife. One habit I inherited from my grandmother Juliet is to buy a small posy of cut flowers every week. They don't have to be grand; more often than not I buy gerberas as they give off oxygen at night which makes them useful plants to have in the bedroom, but tulips or whatever flowers are in season really bring a sense of weekly joy in our home. The key is to buy one variety of flower, or buy one colour—avoid a mix of colours. For the price of a takeaway coffee you have a weekly dose of flower hygge!

# Soft Furnishings & Textiles

As touched on in previous chapters, we Nordics don't fear winter but embrace it. A hallmark of indoor hygge is to recognize that winter is long and dark, so you might as well use the excuse to curl up indoors under a blanket or throw, swaddled in the warmth of a woollen jumper. Throws, sheepskins and cushions in unusual or graphic prints add a specific texture that is integral to Nordic homes. They are an economical way to really soften any interior space and make it a more soothing environment to live in.

# Books

Both Magnus Englund and I share a love of books and agree how odd it is when you visit a home that has no books on display. Books never go out of style, nor does reading for that matter. In Iceland they have a most civilized Christmas tradition and reverence for books that makes any bibliophile's heart sing: *Jólabókaflóðið*, or 'Christmas book flood'. According to NPR, Iceland publishes more books per capita than any other country on earth, with 'five books published for every 1000 Icelanders', and the annual flood of books during the festive season is eagerly anticipated. As a nation, Iceland's love of books and literary tradition has ancient roots, as cited in Charlotte and Peter Fiell's book *Scandinavian Design*:

*'Of the original settlers who began arriving on the island over 1100 years ago, the majority came from Norway and the remainder from other Scandinavian countries, Ireland and Scotland ... The early blending of Nordic and Celtic stock may partly account for the Icelanders' (unique in Scandinavia) production of great medieval literature.'*

If you have limited space to store books think of investing in invisible shelves to screw into walls and use the books as a design feature. The Billy bookcase from IKEA is a favourite for a simple, economical storage solution and, if you have the budget and space, building library structures into your home can add flair. Look at stairwells, dining rooms, and hidden nooks and crannies as spaces to feature books or build mini libraries—they don't all have to remain in the same room. And the easiest way to categorize books if you have lots to display? Always by subject.

# Mixing Old & New

When I was growing up in Norway I didn't anticipate that wooden Fjord cutlery would become quite so coveted today. Originally made for Dansk International Designs (1960) by Jens Quistgaard, these simple designs were just something we had around the house, nothing special. We filled an Iittala Ultima Thule 370mm serving platter with North Sea shrimps when guests came round, and my parents were given an Arabia tableware set in Anemone for their wedding (featured in the image with the blue jumper and mug on page 4). Every year when I was a child, Grandma Johansen would give me a calendar featuring Carl Larsson's illustrations, and that imagery became ingrained without me really understanding how much Larsson's work influenced our design culture. We were surrounded by beautiful Nordic design in our home and in our family, but it wasn't until recently that I fully understood how powerful an influence that visual language was in defining my own aesthetic taste. Thankfully, it's possible to combine these older pieces with new objects and they still look timeless. Mixing old and new fills your home with cherished memories and takes away that sterile feeling when interiors are all brand new.

# Hygge Investment Pieces

If you're thinking long term about how to add a little Nordic design flair to your home, it can be a little daunting when searching on the web. Max Fraser of *London Design Guide* recommended the following:

∞ Designs from littala, particularly the work of Kaj Franck

∞ Most glassware from Orrefors

∞ Furniture from Swedese is elegant and timeless in wood

∞ All of the pieces by Poul Kjaerholm for Fritz Hansen

∞ Hans Wegner

∞ The work of Claesson Koivisto Rune from Sweden

∞ Andreas Engesvik from Norway

∞ Anderssen & Voll; newcomers Vera & Kyte; lighting from Wästberg; the accessible creations from HAY

∞ Handmade glass designs by Ingegerd Råman for Orrefors

∞ The w153 Île clamp lamp by Inga Sempé for Wästberg

And I asked Magnus Englund, if he could choose only three objects of Nordic design which would he invest in?

∞ *Pre-Artek (1935) Alvar Aalto Stools:* These were first released in 1932/3, under the title 'Stool, model no. 60' and are one of the icons of Aalto's vast portfolio of designs. As Magnus rightly points out, they have endless uses: you can use them as a table by your stylish chair, or by your bed. They double as a footstool and they're stackable which means you can keep them safely tucked away and bring them out as extra chairs if someone drops round for an impromptu

dinner. Quintessentially Nordic in their versatility and practical applications, these stools are worth tracking down if you can. Contemporary versions are available too, of course.

∞ *Kaj Franck's Teema tableware range for Iittala* (now), previously made by Arabia (1977–80) and based on the original Kilta series designed in the late 1940s and early 1950s (also Arabia); the latter was originally made of heat-resistant earthenware and issued in a palette of pretty colours that complemented both food and the interiors of Nordic homes. This range has passed the test of time with its simple lines and hard-wearing durability. As Magnus says, 'A plate is a plate is a plate', and I agree. Whereas previous generations would have aspired to a formal dining service plus an everyday one, Franck smashed that old-fashioned idea with his beautiful designs:

" 'Beauty is the harmony of purpose and form'
—— *the Nordic design aesthetic in a nutshell.*"

he saw no need for two sets of tableware. 'It's as if a child drew a plate', according to Magnus, and that's one of the reasons cooks love this range so much: it acts as a blank canvas for food, plus it just works. Beautiful, timeless and hard-wearing—that's a hygge kitchen investment range right there.

∞ *Eero Saarinen's 'Tulip' table (1955–57):* the son of Gottlieb Eliel Saarinen, one of the finest Finnish designers of the twentieth century who launched the Cranbrook Academy, America's leading design school, Eero Saarinen was a Finnish-American architect and designer who fused the humanistic principles of great Nordic design with a mid-century American design aesthetic. Eero wanted to get away from the 'tyranny of chair legs' that bedevils anyone who has ever tried to gather a group around a table with legs. The Tulip table's floating top perched on one solid, central base is so utterly brilliant in its simplicity you wonder why no one thought of it before. This table, whether you opt for a marble top or a white surface, works with everything and epitomizes that Nordic sense of what Aalto called 'harmony of purpose and form'.

It goes without saying that these last three suggestions are not essential to creating hygge at home, but they are listed here to give you an idea of what tastemakers value in Nordic design. The main thing is to keep it simple, and create a space in which you feel calm and a sense of content-ment, one that you can share with friends and family.

After all, as we shall see in the next chapter, hygge is firmly anchored in a spirit of kinship and conviviality ...

∞

Alvar Aalto's Pre-Artek
Stools: endlessly versatile and
practical, they encapsulate the
timelessness of Nordic design

eight
—
kinship,
conviviality
& openness

# Hygge for All

'And above all, watch with glittering eyes the whole world around you because the greatest secrets are always hidden in the most unlikely places. Those who don't believe in magic will never find it.'
Roald Dahl

Throughout this book I've maintained that hygge embodies the very best of Nordic living. We actively choose to make the most of nature, the seasons and the outdoors. We quite like making stuff. Our approach to food and drink can best be described as a culture of healthy hedonism. And Nordic homes are decorated with simplicity; after all, they are places to slow down, to come together or to savour those rare moments of quiet solitude.

Above all, to live a life of hygge requires kindness: kindness to ourselves in the everyday acts that bring contentedness and pleasure, and kindness to others in a spirit of kinship and conviviality. Sharing is caring, the saying goes, and in general people across the Nordic countries value cooperation over isolation. Sceptics of the supposed Nordic 'model' like to point out how high the suicide rates are in the Arctic, how rampant the consumption of antidepressants is in Denmark, or how taciturn and closed off people in the region can be. I'm not disputing any of that—we are imperfect—but to be human is by nature to be imperfect. The idea that we in the Nordic countries somehow have all the solutions to life's problems is just silly. So whenever I encounter critics who dismiss living in the region as deeply flawed and a model of living that can't be replicated elsewhere, I counter with examples I've cited throughout this book and point out how jolly our social occasions are. From animated singing at wedding receptions, to midsummer feasts that mirror Christmas in their importance to the Nordic calendar of annual festivities, and crayfish parties—yes, parties to celebrate crustacea!—the pleasure principle is alive and kicking across the region, and that is at the very heart of hygge.

# Looking Outward

While our Viking ancestors may have had a reputation as fearsome raiders, one positive legacy we've inherited from them is to look outward. As Michael Pye observes in *The Edge of the World: How the North Sea Made Us Who We Are*:

'*Men trapped by long winters, barely scratching a living out of narrow lands, found the sea their obvious escape. They had no great riches to defend at home, no neighbour enemies. They had every reason to move on and on.*'

We know now that the Norsemen made it as far as Constantinople (Istanbul) and North America, and that spirit of pragmatism, of exploration, still lives on today—think of Roald Amundsen's Antarctic expedition and Thor Heyerdahl's *Kon-Tiki* voyage, to name but two examples. A realistic approach to trade and migration is deeply ingrained in countries of a northerly latitude—there are certain things we produce and have in abundance in the Nordic region, but there are many others we don't have and we rely on the outside world to supply us with. Isolation simply wasn't a viable option in the long run, and nor is it now.

Throughout history, trading with other parts of the world was vital, and that is true as much of the Nordic countries as it is of continental Europe, and of the UK. Our region may have been rich in natural resources such as salt cod, metals and wood, but food production was, as Pye notes, at times a real problem. The trade in goods with the outside world not only brought much-needed supplies, but also an exchange of ideas, new skills and tantalizing flavours, as illustrated by one small example I like to use when I'm asked how imported spices can be seen as quintessentially Nordic: In Norway, Bergen's baking culture wouldn't be what it is today without the Hanseatic League. Germanic baking traditions were introduced by Hansa bakers, who settled in the Kontor district of the city and remained there for centuries. Imported traditions became native traditions. Exotic spices such as cinnamon and cardamom became native flavours. Looking outward brought us vital supplies, yes, but also a lasting legacy of delicious *skillingsboller* (in the case of Bergen); *kanelbuller*, or cinnamon buns as they're known in Sweden; *korvapuusti* in Finland; and an entire pantheon of *wienerbrod* or *viennoiserie*, as the Danish tradition of pastries is known. The history of food cultures across the globe tells a similar tale.

Which is why, as a cook, I find the focus on native ingredients, on eschewing imported foods to create a 'pure' Nordic food narrative, a little odd. Why not have both? Lemons and garlic and Mediterranean herbs add so much to any cook's repertoire—why create binary categories of local and 'other'? It doesn't make any sense to me, but then if you recall from chapter three, the Johansen pantry is a thoroughly international one, replete with miso, soy sauce, wasabi, peanut butter, pasta, rice and about a dozen different types of green tea. As we Nordics consume the most coffee, chocolate and Coca-Cola per capita in the world, it feels a little artificial to fetishize indigenous ingredients. Our food culture has long been enriched by looking outward.

# Coming Together

*'If you are more fortunate than others it is better to build a longer table than a taller fence.'*

—                                                                          author unknown

The willingness to look beyond our own borders, to see the world outside as somewhere to explore, not to fear, are for me among some of the best of Nordic qualities. What does that mean in the context of hygge? I reckon an open-mindedness about the world outside can also be applied to the way we live our lives at home. Humans everywhere are social animals and progress by living in communities that allow us the freedom to be who we are, to trust others, to come together. The Nordic tradition of liberalism and tolerance is something most are rightly proud of, and all it takes is a simple word: welcome.

There is something profoundly elemental about the need for kinship and conviviality. By now you'll have surmised that members of this household love to eat. To use Fergus Henderson's memorable phrase (and the title of Adam Gopnik's excellent book): 'The Table Comes First'. Rare was the evening when my parents and I didn't sit down to a meal together. It was a way for us all to digest the day's events, to decompress and to talk through any issues that may have arisen. As restaurants in Oslo were expensive, we usually entertained at home, my mother resorting to her tried and tested method of serving a smörgåsbord of Norwegian seafood, quick pickles, bread, butter and sour cream, along with the requisite bottles of wine and something she called 'boozy fruit

—

salad' (it was the early 1990s after all). Guests appreciated those occasions not just because the food was delicious, but more importantly, once everything was served, my parents could relax as hosts and the conversation flowed. It was as unpretentious as hygge should be—no starched, white tablecloths, no elaborate dining ritual, or fancy cutlery, just old-fashioned hospitality at its best.

If friends from school came round for a sleepover, we kids would be fed a proper meal before we disappeared to watch *Pretty Woman* or *Dirty Dancing*. We enjoyed *fredagskos*, also known as *fredagsmys* in Sweden, during which we'd munch on Haribos and our favourite chocolates to our heart's content, but that was it for the week—all candy and desserts were off the menu during the next six days. It was a prime example of the spirit of 'healthy hedonism' enjoyed by many across the region: eat a little of what you fancy, but not in excess. Moderation is a distinctly unsexy word, but it works.

Eating at a table also taught us kids how to interact with adults. We weren't patronized with a separate menu, and rarely were we indulged with junk food. We ate what the grown-ups ate, and participated in their conversations, which became our conversations too. Whether it was idle gossip or news of current affairs, we were expected to have an opinion on the subjects of the day. Seclusion simply wasn't an option, nor was sitting and eating mindlessly in front of a TV set.

For our family, like many others, solidarity with kith and kin is forged at the table, nourishing us beyond the essential nutrients we are eating. As Michael Pollan has observed, sharing food is often the missing piece in the jigsaw puzzle of why certain populations have greater content-edness and longevity, why the French supposedly don't get fat (hate to break it to you, but some of them do), and why the Italians and Greeks with their Mediterranean diet score so highly on health indexes. It's not merely a love of great bread, cheese, wine, delicious olive oil, spaghetti and fragrant herbs that keeps most people in the Mediterranean from keeling over in their prime—researchers now increasingly acknowledge that the *social context* of eating matters as much as the food we put in our mouths. Eating 'mindfully' may be in vogue in wellbeing circles, but that kind of misses the point: it's the company of *others* that allows you to really savour your food. Plucking random ingredients from other food cultures and scoffing them without an understanding of how that food is consumed, how it is enjoyed, how it provides pleasure for those who eat in a relaxed state of communion with others, is counterproductive, hence

∞

Big platters of food for sharing is how we ate as a family, and I apply the same formula when entertaining now my position throughout this book that Nordic hygge has to be understood in the context of how people live in those countries.

Aside from socializing us, the act of eating together also serves as an incubator for creativity. A free flow of ideas fosters debate thanks to the opportunity to discuss matters in an atmosphere of reason and open-mindedness. As Icelandic artist Olafur Eliasson writes in his introduction to *Studio Olafur Eliasson: The Kitchen*, when the ninety people working in his studio pause at lunchtime:

*'Sitting around one long table, sharing food, we take the opportunity to get inspiration from unexpected corners, while also engaging in pragmatic conversations about work, chitchat, or exchanging the odd piece of gossip.'*

## "The social context of eating matters as much as the food we put in our mouths." ——

For those who think the act of eating is banal, and food is 'just' fuel, Eliasson's lunchtime repasts provide a convincing counterargument. Indeed, as mentioned previously in this book, researchers in Sweden have found that taking fika every day in an office can help boost morale and act as a 'collective restoration' for employees. Hygge is as much about these enlightened ideals, and what some would call 'slow management', as it is about the everyday acts of nurturing and looking after yourself.

Is this unique to the Nordic countries? Of course not. In Spain they engage in *sobremesa*, which literally means 'over the table', referring to the time spent lingering at a table after sharing a meal together. An Iberian version of hygge, if you will. Think about which meals have been the most memorable in your life. I bet at least one of them would involve such a get-together, a gathering around a table in conversation with friends and loved ones, and not necessarily in a fancy restaurant or at an elaborate

—— *"The act of eating together also serves as an incubator for creativity."*

dinner party. During conversations with fellow cooks and food writers, I've noticed that the stories they tell of great meals are often ones in which the food is almost *incidental*; rather it's the kinship generated through conviviality at the table that really matters

Of the many lessons in life I'm grateful to my parents for, the joy of sitting at a table and sharing simple meals with friends, strangers, loved ones tops the list, and that's why cooking is given such prominence in this book. Cooking is for everyone to participate in, and experienced cooks understand this intuitively.

# A Social Leveller

Kinship and conviviality are not merely about the idyll of families cooking and eating together. A meal with perfect strangers can be a revelation, as the mother of a good friend from university told me. Over informal meetings with women of different faiths, she arranged for them to come together over a bite to eat to learn about each other's backgrounds, the way their lives differed, and discovered what they had in common. The simple act of sitting down for a meal with relative strangers is often an eye-opener in itself, something Ebba Åkerman, the founder of United Invitations (unitedinvitations.org), discovered in her native Stockholm. While teaching Swedish to immigrants, Ebba found that her students often felt segregated from Swedish society at large and she wanted to do something to help them. I asked Ebba to elaborate on why she set up United Invitations:

*'I realized how few of my Swedish friends knew an immigrant, and how few of my students knew Swedes. I felt that the political discussion, whether left or right, did not reflect the reality of my students, and I thought that the more people met and had conversations with each other, maybe we could make society better. Many of my students invited me home for dinners, children's birthdays and parties. So the idea really came from them. The way I was included was the way I wish more people were included in Swedish society. So, I asked my students if they would like to have dinner with a Swede, and I asked my friends if they would like to have dinner with someone learning Swedish.'*

The meals were free, the menu was simple and the concept one that can be replicated anywhere, as Ebba helpfully advises on her website,

∞
The most memorable meals are often the ones in which the food is incidental

giving practical tips on 'how to turn strangers into dinner companions'. The idea has grown organically, resulting in 200 dinners in 2014, three times as many the following year, and another 600 throughout Sweden in the first half of 2016:

*'Most of all I believe in the simplicity of the idea ... Similar dinner groups are active around Europe. They are completely independent, but based on the same idea. They are mostly in Germany, but also in Austria, Switzerland, Belgium, Norway, Finland, UK and Greece.'*

It really doesn't take much to make strangers feel welcome, to feel included, and Ebba's generosity of spirit and enthusiasm for bringing people together is emblematic of a Nordic ideal of openness and tolerance. That progressive spirit is one I instantly recognized and identified with. As a student at the International School in Oslo I learnt early on that, no matter how shy and introverted you are (I was both shy *and* painfully introverted), when you're surrounded by people from across the globe, eating meals together is an insight into other cultures. After all, everyone has to eat, and although the flavour of our food choices may vary, it's a simple ice-breaker at any age. It's much harder to fear the 'other' when you're sharing a meal together, as Ebba found:

*'Our theory of change is that we can get around social exclusion and xenophobia by having dinner together. As individuals we don't have the power to legislate but we can create opportunities and invite people to participate, out of free will, curiosity and joy ... If we build our families around the dinner, can we also build our societies around the dinner table?'*
—      'Social Inclusion at the Dinner Table', Geneva Peace Talks 2015

To my mind, Ebba's United Invitations dinners are a modern interpretation of that Nordic spirit of looking outward, of being open to new cultures. But also of an enterprising spirit, a go-getting attitude we commonly associate with somewhere like the US. Some years ago I became increasingly exasperated with how few Nordic restaurants there were in London, so my friend and colleague, Hannah Forshaw, and I decided to host monthly brunches and supper clubs to showcase Nordic hospitality in a convivial setting. The time and costs involved in putting on those events meant they weren't financially viable in the long term, but I have

—— *"It's the kinship generated through conviviality at the table that really matters."*

fond memories of seeing total strangers sitting down together at a long table, some bravely arriving on their own, and by the time we'd served them a cocktail—or what is known in drinks circles as an 'attitude adjuster'—the conversation became animated and everyone relaxed. We received such kind words of gratitude after each event we hosted that it made all the hard work of organizing those meals seem like no work at all. It was our way of sharing hygge in a setting that we all recognize: good, home-cooked food around a table. You rarely experience that kind of conviviality at a restaurant, unless they explicitly pitch themselves as a family-style place where you sit at long tables with others. More's the pity, as you never know who you will meet and the new friendships that might germinate.

That's the spirit of hygge: a belief in the magic of everyday life, choosing hope and a can-do attitude over fear and despair, and making time to be kind, both to yourself and to others. To quote the Barefoot Contessa, one of my favourite food heroines: how easy is that?

∞
Make the table the focal point of social interactions if you can

# How to Hygge—At a Glance

∞ Nature sets the pace across the Nordic region; rather than fight the elements we embrace the sharp contrast of the seasons.

∞ Spending time in nature calms you. It allows you to step back and to reflect on the very essence of what living is about.

∞ Being in nature has proven physical and mental health benefits, so whenever you have the opportunity, get outside and find some hygge in the wild!

∞ The outdoors is always preferable to the gym.

∞ Being active at all ages is essential. Find a sport or activity that you enjoy, and remember: it's about feeling great, not looking a certain way.

∞ The Nordic spirit of self-sufficiency means knowing how to do and make a few useful things.

∞ How to chop wood, how to make a fire, paint a room, cook a delicious meal ... not only are these useful skills, but they can be fun.

∞ Fika: the daily act of collective restoration at work is an enlightened practice in many Swedish companies.

∞ We don't believe in feeling 'guilty' about the food we eat—a little of what you fancy is a way to bring hygge into your day.

∞ Keep food simple and focus on naturally nourishing foods that will sustain you. Slow down to eat; savour those moments during the day when you can enjoy a delicious meal.

∞ We believe that hygge requires only an economy of effort. No need to bust a gut ...

∞ Skål! The pleasure principle is alive and kicking and a spirit of healthy hedonism reigns supreme.

∞ Inebriation is decidedly not the end goal, but alcohol is a great 'attitude adjuster' when consumed in moderation.

∞ Beauty starts in the home, and we believe a hygge home is a fundamental right of everyone.

∞ Nordic homes are minimalist, yet warm. Natural materials add a timeless element to our design.

∞ Being kind isn't just about the self, and those moments of quiet solitude, it's also about spending time with others, about being sociable and taking pleasure in simple things together.

∞ All are welcome!

# Index

# Further Reading
# & Nordic Resources

From the outset I've tried to steer clear of anything too dry and academic when it comes to the subject of Nordic living and hygge, but the following books have been inspirational in their own way. They don't all relate to hygge as such, but they provide further food for thought if you'd like to read more around the themes raised in this book.

## General Reading

∞  Diane Ackerman, *A Natural History of the Senses*
    (Vintage Books, 1992)
∞  Michael Booth, *The Almost Nearly Perfect People: Behind the
    Myth of the Scandinavian Utopia* (Vintage Books, 2015)
∞  Charlotte and Peter Fiell, *Scandinavian Design*
    (Taschen GmbH, 2013)
∞  Tristan Gooley, *The Natural Navigator*
    (Virgin Books, 2014)
∞  Yuval Noah Harari, *Sapiens: A Brief History of Humankind*
    (Vintage Books, 2015)
∞  Alexandra Heminsley, *Running Like a Girl*
    (Windmill Books, 2014)
∞  Anna Kessel, *Eat Sweat Play*
    (Macmillan, 2016)
∞  Zach Klein and Steven Leckart, *Cabin Porn*
    (Particular Books, 2015)
∞  Aldo Leopold, *A Sand County Almanac*
    (OUP, USA, 1968)
∞  Robert Macfarlane, *The Old Ways: A Journey on Foot*
    (Penguin Books, 2013)
∞  Marcel Mauss, *The Gift*
    (Martino Fine Books, 2011)

∞ Lars Mytting, *Norwegian Wood: Chopping, Stacking and Drying Wood the Scandinavian Way* (MacLehose Press, 2015)

∞ Robert Penn, *The Man Who Made Things Out of Trees* (Penguin Books, 2016)

∞ Michael Pye, *The Edge of the World: How the North Sea Made Us Who We Are* (Penguin Books, 2015)

∞ Richard Sennett, *Together* (Penguin Books, 2013) and *The Craftsman* (Penguin Books, 2009)

∞ Simon Singh, *Fermat's Last Theorem* (Fourth Estate, 2002)

∞ Henry David Thoreau, *Walden; or, Life in the Woods* (Princeton University Press, 2016)

∞ Elizabeth Wilhide, *Scandinavian Modern Home* (Quadrille Publishing, 2008)

∞ Damon Young, *How to Think about Exercise* (Macmillan, 2014)

∞ Theodore Zeldin, *An Intimate History of Humanity* (Vintage Books, 1995)

# Food & Cooking

∞ Darina Allen, *Forgotten Skills of Cooking* (Kyle Cathie, 2009)

∞ Laurie Colwin, *Home Cooking* (Fig Tree, 2012)

∞ Alan Davidson, *North Atlantic Seafood* (Prospect Books, 2012)

∞ Olafur Eliasson, *Studio Olafur Eliasson: The Kitchen* (Phaidon Press, 2016)

∞ Adam Gopnik, *The Table Comes First* (Vintage Books, 2012)

∞ Sandor Ellix Katz, *The Art of Fermentation* (Chelsea Green Publishing Co, 2012)

∞ Mark Kurlansky, *Cod* (Vintage Books, 1999)

∞ Richard Mabey, *Food for Free* (Collins, 2012)

- ∞ Harold McGee, *McGee on Food & Cooking*
  (Hodder & Stoughton, 2004)
- ∞ Bee Wilson, *First Bite*
  (Fourth Estate, 2015)

The books by Diana Henry, Fiona Beckett, Claudia Roden, Nigella Lawson, Richard Bertinet, Tim Hayward, Nigel Slater, Alice Waters, The Barefoot Contessa, Yotam Ottolenghi, Nick Barnard of Rude Health and the *Cook's Illustrated* series of cookbooks have all proven invaluable.

# Nordic Resources

- ∞ The Scandinavian Kitchen, Ocado, Waitrose for ingredients cited in this book. IKEA also does a decent line of Nordic foods
- ∞ Peter's Yard for the best sourdough crispbread (it should be in every kitchen cupboard for impromptu hygge and fika!)
- ∞ Fabrique Bakery for bread and buns
- ∞ Skandium and Att Pynta for design and interiors
- ∞ Hus & Hem, Cloudberry Living for Nordic interiors
- ∞ Iittala, Marimekko, Georg Jensen
- ∞ Hay, Broste Copenhagen, Nordic Elements
- ∞ Although not Nordic, Muji has a similar, spare style that works well with Nordic design and interiors
- ∞ Cos, H&M, Acne, & Other Stories do great Nordic-style basics

# About the Author

After graduating with a Bachelor's degree in archaeology and anthropology from the University of Cambridge, Norwegian-American writer Signe Johansen trained at Leiths School of Food and Wine in London, worked in several of the UK's top restaurants and went on to do her Masters in the anthropology of food at SOAS food studies centre at the University of London. Two critically acclaimed 'Scandilicious' books on Scandinavian food followed, along with contributions to twelve other books on food and restaurants. Signe's writing has appeared in all major UK media publications and she is the co-founder of Spirited Women. Aside from sharing the secrets of hygge here, Signe's in her element when spending time in nature and travelling, and loves trying new outdoor pursuits ...

Follow Signe on social media: *@SigneSJohansen* on Twitter and *SigneSJohansen* on Instagram

# Acknowledgements

This book would never have come about if it hadn't been for a few glasses of wine at Noble Rot Bar with my agent Sarah Williams of the Sophie Hicks Agency. *Tusen takk!*

The *How to Hygge* team have been brilliant at every stage of the book production process, so thank you to Carole Tonkinson, Olivia Morris, Lorraine Jerram, Justine Anweiler, Jodie Mullish, Jessica Farrugia, Charlotte Heal, Linda Berlin, Alice Hart, Nadira V Persaud, Keiko Oikawa for all your hard work in getting this book from a PowerPoint proposal to the finished article. My thanks also to Jane Cumberbatch and your beautiful location house.

The following gave their advice and thoughts on hygge without hesitation: Magnus Englund of Skandium, Sara Malm, Dr Tracy Cox, Charlene Hutsebaut, Diana Henry, Ebba Akerman, Max Fraser, Kell and Jacqueline Skott, Kai Price and Amanda Nelson of Att Pynta.

Niamh Shields, Elana Wilson Rowe, Richard Gray, Lynne Clark, Natacha Catalino, WenLin Soh, Kavita Favelle, Claire Nelson, Jeanne Horak-Druiff, Catherine Phipps, Mimi Aye, Damian Barr, Elissa McGee, Louise Marston, John Shields, Annie Gray, Felicity Spector, Richard Bertinet, Katie Brewis, Johan Duramy, Matt Smith, Rebecca Bevington-Smith—my thanks to you all for sharing your thoughts on life skills. Jason Alexander's dossier on slow management made for fascinating reading.

Thank you to family and colleagues who have been supportive and fun to chat to about food, life and whisky: Fiona Beckett, Aaron and Carolyn Rosen, Nina Kadan, Maunika Gowardhan, Kaitlin Solimine, Camilla Barnard, Judy Joo, Hannah Forshaw, Gabrielle Hales, Dana Elemara, Alexandra Heminsley, Ailana Kamelmacher, Sarah Brown, Rachel McCormack, Annie Gray, Denise Medrano, Debora Richardson, Thane Prince, Sarah Chamberlain, Jon Spiteri, Kay Plunkett-Hogge, Lorne and Amy Somerville, Persephone Books, the BOOM Cycle crew, and the Soho Farmhouse squad: James Lindon, Sasha Morgan and Mungo Wenban-Smith—I may be a disaster on the crazy-golf course but there's no one else in the world I'd rather humiliate myself in front of. And to members of 39 Essex Chambers for tasting and giving feedback on a lot of the cakes in this book.

Last but not least: all my love to Jane Emerald Alexander and Jan Skaimsgard Johansen, quite simply the best parents, who taught me everything I know about How to Hygge.

To Fiona Beckett, a spirited woman and fellow breakfast fiend

∞

*Clockwise from top left:*
*Cross-country skiing with my mother in Oslo;*
*my Norwegian great-uncle Per catching a*
*salmon; and Papa Johansen downhill skiing.*

First published 2016 by Bluebird
an imprint of Pan Macmillan
20 New Wharf Road, London N1 9RR
Associated companies throughout the world
www.panmacmillan.com

ISBN  978-1-5098-3486-0

Image Credits:
Alamy  p. 178; Jonas Anhede pp. 8–9, 26–7, 28, 34, 48; Author's own pp. 31, 38, 207; Linus Englund pp. 10, 14;
Getty Images pp. 19, 46–7, 180–1; Beth Kirby pp. 187, 188, 192; Louise Ljunberg p. 60; Erik von Otto p. 2; Holly Marder pp. 160,
164, 171, 172, 182, 200-201; Morten Nordstrøm p. 41; Andrea Papini p. 194

Printed in Italy

Pan Macmillan does not have any control over, or any responsibility for, any author
or third-party websites referred to in or on this book.

9 8 7 6 5 4 3 2 1

A CIP catalogue record for this book is available from the British Library.

**Publisher** Carole Tonkinson
**Project Editor** Lorraine Jerram
**Art Direction & Design** CHD
**Prop Styling** Linda Berlin
**Food Styling** Alice Hart

Visit **www.panmacmillan.com** to read more about all our books and to buy them. You will also find
features, author interviews and news of any author events, and you can sign up for e-newsletters
so that you're always first to hear about our new releases.